Professor Errare Presents....

46 Jerks and Counting

Professor Errare
and
S. Will Campbell

Published by Shawn Campbell

Professor Errare Presents....46 Jerks and Counting

3rd Edition

ISBN: 978-1-7332314-7-3

To Herodotus, for proving to the world that fact finding is not necessarily a necessity for writing history.

A Note to the Reader

This book should be considered a form of parody and satire created for reasons of entertainment only. In other words, only an idiot would use this book for any type of serious citation. While Professor Errare strives to only provide factual information on the people who have served as the president of the United States, his research methods are somewhat questionable given that each president only got about an hour's worth of internet searching. As well, at times certain facts have been written about in a manner, which while entertaining, may have twisted and stretched the truth just a bit.

This is of course not to say that all of the people who served as president were not jerks in some way, they all most certainly were. You don't reach the office of president if you're not a jerk. This is simply to say that if you find anything in this book of interest, Professor Errare strongly encourages you to do your own research. The internet represents the greatest source of knowledge in human history, maybe try using it for more than cat videos and porn, and of course, cat porn videos.

Finally, this book is not supposed to be a reflection of whether or not each individual was a great president. This book makes no attempt to even look into the policies and accomplishments of each president. Professor Errare is a-political. He does not care about such things. He trusts you to use your own judgment and to be enough of an adult to realize that if you laugh at 45 of these entries and get pissed at one, then you are a hypocritical asshole. There are no golden calves for Professor Errare. All presidents are judged equally as the jerks they all were.

Now that we have the "please don't sue me" stuff out of the way. Here we go....

#1 George Washington
(1789-1797)
America's Giant Made Up God

The original GW was a monstrously tall pox scarred man with hippopotamus teeth, an apparent hatred of cherry trees, and a larger than average member (why else do you think his monument looks like that). This "monumental member" allowed him to marry Martha Dandridge, whose vast family fortune allowed GW to spend most of his time hunting tail (foxtail that is), going to cockfights, holding lavish parties, and in general avoiding poor people whenever possible. GW enjoyed a reputation as a war hero. A reputation he earned in the French and Indian War by getting a third of his men slaughtered in a series of battles, one of which involved an accidental skirmish with his own allies, and by sucking up to the British generals who were his commanding officers.

During the Revolutionary War GW became a patriot because he basically hated paying his taxes. When war broke out, GW was made commander in chief of the army simply because he was the only man who showed up to the meeting in a military uniform. In this capacity he led the Continental Army through many glorious retreats. GW didn't let his lack of success get him down though; to help himself feel better he spent $7.6 million (in today's money) on booze and parties. However, GW didn't forget about the common soldier either. When the Continental Army settled in for winter camp at Valley Forge, he spent a large amount of cash to put on a nice theatrical play to help distract them from the fact they were starving and freezing to death.

After the war, GW got himself elected the first president of the newly created United States by using reverse psychology and pretending he did not want to be president. This was made easier by the fact that all the people who did want to be president were considered assholes. GW really didn't do much as president, but every little day to day thing he did became tradition since he was the first. Life did get exciting when GW decided to use his new found power to tax whiskey, a move which angered the all important drunkard voting bloc. When the aforementioned drunks started an armed rebellion against the U.S. government, GW personally led troops into battle against them to prove that at age 59 he was still a bad ass.

After two terms as president, GW went back to farming hemp. GW died because he went horseback riding in the freezing rain and was too stubborn to change into dry clothes when he got home. This resulted in him getting a bad sore throat, which his old timey doctors tried to cure by removing half of his blood. It was a different time. Upon GW's death, Martha burned all of their correspondence because apparently it was too sexy or something. Over time people turned GW into some kind of godlike folk hero, who is sure to rise from the dead and kick some ass if America is ever in dire need.

#2 John Adams
(1797-1801)
The Pouting Potato

Johnny was a short, squat man who was the first lawyer to be president, starting a precedent that we could have really done without. Johnny was a bookish child, which is a polite way to say he was a bit of a dork who had the social skills of a farting orangutan. However, even nerds rebel, and for Johnny that meant secretly writing essays under the pseudonym Humphrey Ploughjogger and marrying his hot third cousin, Abigail Smith, probably to save on wedding expenses. Johnny had to be careful with his money; he was a middle class misfit running in upper class circles, a fact that never ceased to bother him.

Johnny first rose to prominence when he defended the British soldiers who perpetrated the Boston Massacre, a decision he made purely for the money and exposure. During the Revolutionary War, Johnny worked 18 hour days doing pretty much all of the tedious paper pusher type of stuff that everyone else found really boring. While others were writing the Declaration of Independence, he was filling out forms in triplicate to make sure the Army had enough socks. Doing such thankless tasks made Johnny feel as though he was a vital part of the war effort. Everyone else considered him pretty dull and often described him as a fat little vain obnoxious bitch (but of course in fancy old timey terms).

In 1796, Johnny got himself elected president by running on the platform that his opponent, and former best friend, Thomas Jefferson, was an immoral twat who probably drowned kittens or something along those lines. Once elected, Johnny went all sorts of crazy, forcing people to call him "His Highness" and making it pretty much illegal to disagree with him in anyway. Acting like a crazy dictator did not go over well for some reason, and strangely Johnny was not re-elected in 1800. After losing, Johnny refused to go to Thomas Jefferson's inauguration, instead sneaking out of Washington DC at four in the morning.

After his presidency, Johnny spent most of his time writing essays and letters to his pen pals to refute the mean things Alexander Hamilton had said about him nine years earlier. It should probably be mentioned that at this point Alexander Hamilton had been dead for five years. Amazingly, writing what amounted to angry letters to the editor did not pay well, and Johnny became a pauper in his old age, dependent upon his children for money. Johnny died of heart failure, which was probably totally unrelated to the fact that the man resembled a walking potato.

#3 Thomas Jefferson
(1801-1809)
The Eccentric Mumbling Genius

Jeffy, who was also a lawyer, was some kind of eccentric genius who loved science and reading. Like many famous men of his time, he married his hot third cousin, Martha Skelton, which just so happened to also double his land and wealth. Jeffy then proceeded to lose all of his wealth building a ridiculously large house called Monticello. When Martha died young, she forced Jeffy to promise never to remarry. Jeffy, an outside the box type of thinker, solved this unfortunate situation by sexing it up with one of his own slaves, Sally Hemmings, who also happened to be his wife's half-sister.

Jeffy was widely considered to be a weird dude, even for someone who devotes their life to politics. He would often come to meetings dressed in a fashion similar to Liberace (if Liberace was a hobo), wearing his bedroom slippers, with a mockingbird sitting and shitting on his shoulder. A shy man, Jeffy avoided eye contact with those around him, mumbled when spoken to, and was easily startled by loud noises. This was the man who wrote the Declaration of Independence, but more importantly, this was the man who invented the swivel chair.

In 1800, Jeffy got elected president by being less of an asshole than President Johnny, a feat that couldn't have been that hard to do. For his inauguration he was presented with a 1,200 pound cheese, which he left in the White House until it stunk up the joint. Jeffy's presidency was a random collection of crazy shit. Jeffy doubled the size of the country by buying Louisiana from France, fought a war with pirates in North Africa, and dealt with his former Vice President, Aaron Burr, who was conspiring to create some kind of personal kingdom out west. Just to keep things as weird as possible, Jeffy kept a sheep at the White House which was widely believed to be possessed by the devil or something along those lines. The sheep would often attack visitors, and even killed a young boy.

Despite owning a killer sheep, Jeffy was re-elected in 1804. He then pretty much checked out and let his subordinates do all the work while he went back to expanding and refurbishing his already ridiculous house. This never ending project drove him into poverty. Jeffy's presidency made him quite famous, and throughout his retirement unwanted guests would come to visit, treating the poor shy man as though he were some kind of zoo exhibit. As Jeffy got older he developed rheumatism, which he treated by visiting hot springs. This resulted in him getting a terrible ass infection, which his old timey doctors treated with mercury. This of course led to mercury poisoning, the treatment for which resulted in him getting a kidney infection, which in turn finally killed him off.

#4 James Madison
(1809-1817)
A Tiny Man With A Hot Wife

Jemmy, as he was called by his jerky friends and family, was an extremely tiny man. I cannot overemphasize how tiny he was. We're talking about 5 foot 4, 100 pounds sopping wet. We're talking so tiny he tried to join the army during the Revolutionary War and was told he was too tiny. Jemmy didn't help his shortcomings at all by being a huge nerd. He went to university, where unsure what to do with his life, he just studied everything. Jemmy was a studying machine. He studied so long and hard that he actually damaged his health. Oh yeah, he just wasn't tiny, he was also sickly. The man was sick all the time. Like constant tummy troubles and epileptic fits sick. Jemmy was just a tiny, delicate little dude.

Not being big enough to fight, Jemmy instead got involved in politics and heavy drinking, though to be fair, at the time you really couldn't do one without the other. After the Revolutionary War, Jemmy did help write one famous document. Perhaps you've heard of it: the U.S. Constitution. Not impressed? You try designing a government while you're drunk, have constant diarrhea, keep passing out for no good reason, and your asshole friends keep making short jokes behind your back. Like most nerds, Jemmy had to wait until he was successful later in life to get married. Of course, when he did, it was to a hot piece of ass 17 years his junior, a widower named Dolley Todd.

Jemmy was elected president in 1808 because President Jeffy told everyone to vote for him and because everyone thought his wife Dolley was just the coolest. Seriously, there are entire books written on how awesome and fabulously popular Dolley was. In 1812, the US got involved in the creatively named War of 1812. To this day no one really has any to clue to why. It was probably the most pointless war in history. We burned down some buildings in Canada, the British burned down the White House, that was about it. Of course, what do you expect with tiny little Jemmy in power? It wouldn't be hard to imagine some Napoleon Complex aspect to the whole thing (though given Napoleon was still alive at the time they probably called it something else). New England also tried to secede from the union during his tenure, so you know, Jemmy wasn't doing all that great of a job.

After his presidency, Jemmy retired to his plantation, Montpelier, where he sat around playing chess, reading Latin, and slowly going broke. As he got older, Jemmy became super paranoid about his legacy. He got so paranoid that he went all Joseph Stalin on his letters and diaries, changing everything that might in any way make him look bad, so you know, pretty much everything. Lifting that heavy pen must have been pretty rough on his delicate little body, as Jemmy eventually died of heart failure.

#5 James Monroe
(1817-1825)
The Insane Hipster

In 1776, Mad Jimmy dropped out of law school to join the Continental Army in the Revolutionary War. There he served as a scout for many major battles, gaining the reputation for being a half crazed bad ass. We can't prove that Mad Jimmy once bit a British soldier's face off, but we can't disprove it either. After the war, Mad Jimmy got heavily involved in politics, serving in some type of office for the rest of his life, probably because it was easier than having a real job. All his politicking caught the eye of Elizabeth Kortright, a well known babe who was so hot that she once interrupted an entire play just by entering the theater. Mad Jimmy of course married her, and then celebrated his nuptials by honeymooning on Long Island, which was apparently super romantic at the time, and then opposing the ratification of the U.S. Constitution.

Mad Jimmy was elected president by a landslide in 1816 because the opposing party, instead of having the balls to run a nominee against him, instead decided to just fold up and quit existing. In 1820, he ran unopposed again, so was unsurprisingly re-elected. Mad Jimmy was a bit of an unconventional politician. He was well known for chasing his cabinet members around the White House with a pair of fire tongs when he got angry, and he always wore clothes that were at least thirty years out of date. Mad Jimmy was pretty much the last guy in America to still wear powdered wigs, knee breeches, and those funky shoes with the big buckles on them. In other words, Mad Jimmy was exactly like that uncle of yours who still wears polyester suits.

Despite his shortcomings, Mad Jimmy did know how to get shit done. In 1819, he bought Florida from Spain, probably just because he thought it would be funny if the map of the U.S.A. looked like it had a penis. He was also the first president to ride in a steamboat, which is something, we guess, and he created the Monroe Doctrine, which basically told Europe to keep their dirty fingers out of the business of all the new nations in the Americas, because, by god, if anyone was going to screw them up, it was going to be Mad Jimmy and the good old U.S. of A.

After his presidency, Mad Jimmy retired to Virginia, where, like most of his predecessors, he did his best to go completely broke. Martha, who despite being a total babe, was never really the picture of health, which drove Mad Jimmy further into insolvency. When she died, he became severely depressed and moved in with his daughter in New York City. There, he died of tuberculosis and heart failure. Though truth to be told, he missed his wife so much that he probably actually died of a broken heart.......and tuberculosis.

#6 John Quincy Adams
(1825-1829)
Friend Of The Mole People

Potato Junior was the son of President Johnny. He was given the middle name Quincy because that was the name of the town he was born in. His parents were not creative people. Potato Junior spent most his childhood travelling the world and later became a diplomat for the United States, something for which he undoubtedly always found reasons to bring up at parties. Potato Junior was not a happy man. He was constantly mopey and depressed, probably because his failure of a father put a lot of pressure on him to be a success. This may be the reason why Potato Junior couldn't find a wife in America. To solve the problem, his mother forced him to marry a British woman named Louisa Johnson, who had the reputation of being kind of a pain in the ass.

Because his father was always too busy being all political to ever pay attention to him, Potato Junior did his best to gain his father's approval by being every bit as successful. This led to Potato Junior being elected president in 1824. His father showed his approval by dying soon after. The election of 1824 was very contentious, with Andrew Jackson winning the majority of the popular vote, but not the electoral vote. This resulted in the House of Representatives electing Potato Junior as president because old timey politics were just as screwed up as today's politics.

Making Potato Junior president was probably a mistake. The man gave all signs of being certifiably crazy. Though he was good at making speeches, he pretty much did jack shit as president. Potato Junior had the strange habit of swimming naked in the Potomac River. This activity led to him being the first president ever interviewed by a woman, a feat accomplished after the aforementioned woman stole his clothes. Probably the craziest thing Potato Junior ever did was try to fund an expedition to the North Pole where he was certain a secret entrance to the interior of the Earth would be found. The expedition would be expensive, but it would be totally worth it when it opened up lucrative trade with the mole people.

In 1828, Potato Junior followed in his father's footsteps by failing to get re-elected. He lost to Andrew Jackson because people thought Andrew Jackson was the least crazy of the two, and that's really saying something. After his presidency, Potato Junior got himself elected to the House of Representatives where he spent his time making angry speeches and generally ignoring his family in much the same way his own father had ignored him. During a vote on honoring veterans of the Mexican War, which Potato Junior was strongly against, he loudly screamed, "No," suffered a stroke, and died. Historians later agreed that having a stroke was a rather brilliant, but poorly executed, debate tactic.

#7 Andrew Jackson
(1829-1837)
How In The Hell Was This Man Elected President?

It just has to be said up front, AJ was fucking crazy. Orphaned at a young age, AJ decided to become a lawyer, but instead of bothering with all that fancy schooling, he just taught himself how to do it. This was the norm for his entire life. When AJ met the still married, but separated, Rachel Robards, he said fuck it again, and married her too. When people started bad mouthing his marital choice, he started challenging them to duels. How many duels do you ask? Somewhere around 100, all of which he won. When shooting people got boring, AJ ran for Congress, got elected, and then quit after a year because he got bored of that too. None of these facts describe a man that could be called sane.

AJ was a tall skinny man who was constantly coughing up blood due to the several musket balls lodged in his chest. Inheriting a princely sum from his grandfather, he quickly lost it all betting on horse races. When AJ lacked money to pay his gambling debts, he solved the problem by fighting in a duel. Not finding enough random people to shoot via dueling, AJ joined the army and became a general in the War of 1812, where he became a national hero by winning the Battle of New Orleans with a random army of volunteers and pirates. Sure, the war had been over for 15 days, but AJ was never a man to let little details like that stop him. Following the War of 1812, AJ spent his time attacking various native tribes, adopting two native children that he had just made orphans, and then invading Florida, because why the hell not.

In 1828, AJ was elected president after a down and dirty mudslinging campaign. The opposition claimed that AJ's wife, Rachel, was a bigamist, which was a polite old timey way to say slut. The stress of the election ruined Rachel's health and she died soon after AJ became president. This of course made him go even crazier. How crazy? So crazy he forced all the native tribes east of the Mississippi to move to Oklahoma. So crazy that when an even crazier man tried to assassinate him, he nearly beat the man to death with his cane. So crazy that he left a 1,400 pound cheese to rot in the White House front hall for three years. So crazy the White House had more keggers than a frat house. So crazy that when South Carolina threatened to secede he gave them the crazy eye until they backed down.

After his presidency, AJ retired to his plantation in Tennessee where he spent most of his time betting on cockfights and generally just getting crazier and crotchetier. Despite rumors that AJ was immortal, he died of dropsy, tuberculosis, and heart failure, because just one ailment wasn't enough. At his funeral, AJ's pet parrot had to be removed from the church because it wouldn't stop cursing. It's said that if you say AJ's name three times in a darkened room his ghost will appear and shoot your ass.

#8 Martin Van Buren
(1837-1841)
The Prissy Troll

Old K was a short troll like man who couldn't grow hair on the top of his head, so instead grew it in copious amounts on the sides of his face. Old K was born in Kinderhook, New York, and was given the nickname Old Kinderhook (which led to the phrase OK), because people were crazy creative back then. Though in retrospect, it was better than his other nicknames, which included Little Van, Martin Van Ruin, Blue Whiskey Van (because he was a drunk), and the Little Magician. As with many presidents, he was a lawyer who married his hot first cousin, Hannah Hoes, because if you're going to marry your cousin, it better not be the one with the good personality. Unlike other presidents, Old K's first language was Dutch.

When he was younger, Old K was known for being a shitty dresser, wearing nothing but homespun, which was the JC Penney of the 19th century. After some friends suggested he try dressing better, he swung the pendulum completely to the other side, wearing frilly clothes with bows and ribbons. When Old K's wife died young, he decided against remarrying, probably because he was all out of hot cousins, and instead went into politics, becoming the right hand man of crazy ass President AJ. This led him to becoming Vice President, a job he hated so much that he carried live pistols to Senate meetings and often pretended to have a severe cold so he wouldn't have to attend.

In 1836, Old K was elected president because Crazy Ass Jackson told everyone to vote for him or get shot in a duel. Old K evidently got confused, thinking president meant king. After he was elected, he started riding around in gilded carriages and using only golden dinnerware. He also kept two tiger cubs at the White House and pretty much forced the king of the Netherlands to give him a noble coat of arms. Given that the country was in the middle of an economic depression at the time, this made Old K less than popular. Even keeping Canada from starting a war over Maine couldn't save his popularity. As happens to many people, the stress made Old K gain weight, a fact he hid by wearing a corset.

Thrown out of office after only one term, Old K returned to Kinderhook, where he got gouty and gassy, and worked on his 776 page autobiography which was notable for never mentioning his wife or the fact that he was once the president. Old K also passed the time by running for president three more times, losing every single time. Old K died by suffocating to death. The doctors claimed it was due to asthma, though it was more likely because the fat bastard refused to loosen his god damn corset.

#9 William Henry Harrison
(1841)
Too Old To Be President

Tippy was born to a wealthy plantation family where he spent his time doing rich plantation stuff, such as knocking up enslaved women. Tiring of these shenanigans, Tippy's family sent him to medical school, but like so many rich kids, he soon dropped out and became a deadbeat. Embarrassed, his family convinced him to join the military where he was sent to the frontier to fight the natives. It was here that he met Anna Symmes, a woman who had a lot going for her: she was well educated, easy on the eyes, and her family was wealthy. So of course, like many women who have a lot going for them, she decided to marry a deadbeat despite her family's protests.

Though a deadbeat, Tippy did prove to be rather good at fighting the natives of the frontier. In fact, he slaughtered a whole village of them at Tippencanoe, earning the nickname Old Tippencanoe, again, because people were super creative back then, and also because old timey folks were just the worst. Somehow, slaughtering women and children translated into getting into politics, which resulted in Tippy getting elected a frontier governor. He then retired to help invade Canada during the War of 1812, and then became a member of Congress for a while before retiring because he was getting pretty damned old.

In 1840, people noticed that, similar to Crazy Ass Jackson, Tippy was a general with a silly nickname who hated Natives Americans, and decided that was a good enough reason to have him run for president. Tippy, thanks to his rich upbringing, was an aristocratic gentleman who liked to sip wine and talk about the finer things in life. To make him more likable to the general hillbilly population, his campaign claimed that he lived in a log cabin and spent most of his time drinking hard cider from a jug. The ruse, combined with his campaign of handing out free booze, worked, and Tippy was elected president.

Tippy was an old man when he was elected president. Old as balls. But to prove he was healthy as a horse, Tippy gave the longest inauguration speech in U.S. history, in the freezing rain, with no gloves, hat, or coat. Unsurprisingly, Tippy got a fever which his old timey doctors treated with the best medicine of the day: opium, enemas, and leeches. Despite the miracles of modern medicine, Tippy died after being president only 33 days.

#10 John Tyler
(1841-1845)
The Human Buzzard

Jay Ty was a little man (funny how so many of these guys were little) who resembled some kind of sickly vulture. A sickly vulture that suffered from constant diarrhea throughout its life. He was born to an aristocratic plantation family and studied economics and law, becoming a lawyer when he was only 19. When he wasn't studying, Jay Ty took up the common plantation owner hobby of impregnating his slaves, but Jay Ty added his own little twist, selling his bastard children to other plantations. When ruining the lives of enslaved people got too boring, he got married to a woman named Letitia Christian and pumped out eight legitimate children.

Jay Ty never really wanted to be in politics, but his family and friends kept pushing him into it and he was too much of a sissy to just say no. This resulted in him becoming Vice President in 1841. Not really wanting to be Vice President, Jay Ty took the mature route of just not showing up to work, staying home at his plantation. However, President Tippy cleverly thwarted Jay Ty's plan by immediately dying. At the time there were no real rules for what would happen if the president died. Jay Ty solved the problem by moving his shit into the White House and declaring himself president, which he apparently thought meant dictator. This marked the first time a person had become president without ever being elected.

Jay Ty's ascendency to the presidency made his wife, Letitia, so happy that she just up and died. Feeling that he did not yet have enough kids, Jay Ty got remarried to a woman named Julia Gardiner, who, as befitting a man in a powerful position, was 30 years his junior. Julia was a bit of a firecracker. She had been a controversial model in New York, getting her picture taken for a clothing store ad with a man who was not a relative (the horror). Her appalled family had sent her to Europe to make her more of a conservative lady, which even back then did not make a bit of sense.

Jay Ty was not a popular president. He never had a Vice President (given his own method of becoming president, who could blame him), his entire cabinet resigned en masse, his own political party disowned him, several attempts were made to impeach him, and he was often called the least popular man in America (which given the times was no small feat). Unsurprisingly, Jay Ty failed to win re-election in 1845.

After leaving the presidency, Jay Ty moved back to his plantation and pumped out seven more kids with his hot young wife. His neighbors, being assholes, put him charge of keeping the local road in good condition. Jay Ty kept that damn road in pristine order. When the Confederacy seceded from the Union, Jay Ty made a comeback and got himself elected to the Confederate Congress. Before he could take office, he came down with a severe cold, claimed he felt dizzy, vomited, had a drink of brandy, and died. At his death, the United States declared Jay Ty a traitor and refused to hold a state funeral. Jay Ty's wife, Julia, later claimed she had dreamed of her husband's death before it happened. History does not record whether or not she considered it a good dream or a bad dream.

#11 James K. Polk
(1845-1849)
It Has Nothing To Do With My Non-Working Balls

Pokey had beetle brows and crazy eyes and probably never lost a staring contest. As a child, Pokey never went to school because he was always sick with gall stones. This situation was solved at age 17 when a doctor gave him a swig of brandy, and then while he was still awake, cut him open and removed the troubling stones. The surgery was a success, in that it made Pokey healthy enough to attend school, but it also made him sterile, which was less than optimal. Pokey didn't let his relative lack of education and non-working balls slow him down though. He made up for his lack of book smarts by marrying Sarah Childress, a woman chock full of them to the brim.

With the help of his super smart wife, Pokey became a lawyer and bought a farm for himself which he cleverly named Polk Place, a name which probably led to a lot of confused illiterate drunks showing up to his door looking for a brothel. With his wife writing all his speeches, Pokey got into politics, earning himself a nickname, Young Hickory, because he was pretty much Crazy Ass Jackson's bottom bitch. In 1844, he ran for president with a campaign of no one having any idea who he was, making him the most likable candidate. It didn't hurt either that he was the youngest man to ever run, something of importance given what had happened to President Tippy. It was a winning combination.

Pokey's genius wife, Sarah, was uber religious. When the couple moved into the White House, she banned liquor, cards, dancing, and probably even laughter. Pokey was a hard working son of a bitch, though given that his wife hated fun, it was not like he had anything better to do. Pokey decided that it was time for the U.S. to start kicking ass and taking names. Territory names that is. He went to war against Mexico, claiming all of what is today the southwestern U.S.A., a move that could be best compared to an adult beating up a kindergartner for a piss flavored lollipop covered with dirt. In truth, Pokey probably just wanted California, but wisely took the rest so the U.S. didn't look like it had another dick on maps. Pokey also annexed the Oregon Country and Texas, and even tried unsuccessfully to buy Cuba from Spain. When Pokey wasn't busy making the U.S. bigger, he mostly spent his time letting random people into the White House to chat and also writing detailed descriptions in his diary of his constant diarrhea.

After only one term, Pokey announced that he would retire rather than run again. He was in pretty poor health, what with all the diarrhea, and most people agreed that he looked like shit, exhausted from overwork, and unable to relax because his wife had banned everything even remotely fun, except maybe for constantly shitting. Hell, the woman probably banned smiles. Three months after leaving the presidency, Pokey visited New Orleans, contracted cholera, and died. Historians generally agree that while bad, cholera was relatively better than the things most people contracted in New Orleans.

#12 Zachary Taylor
(1849-1850)
The Amazing Spitting Frog

Imagine a frog in a general's uniform. You are now picturing Zachary Taylor. Zack was born out on the frontier in a log cabin and had no time for book learning. He had more important things to do, such as chewing tobacco and practicing his spitting. Who cares if even as an adult his handwriting and grammar skills resembled that of a six year old? Who cares that he sometimes misspelled his own name? I'll tell you who didn't care, the man who could hit a spittoon at thirty paces every god damn time, that's who.

With very few career options available, what with being an illiterate spittle covered buffoon, Zack joined the Army, a career choice he was surprisingly good at. Over time he rose through the ranks, battling the Brits in the War of 1812 and kicking natives off their ancestral homelands. It was in these early years that Zack married Margaret Smith, a peculiarly reclusive woman who for some reason promised god that she would avoid people if Zack didn't get killed while at war. Zack became a famous general following the Mexican War, earning himself the nickname Old Rough and Ready, which seems strange given that the man always rode side saddle. Hoping to cash in on his war hero status, numerous groups tried to convince Zack to run for president. Zack eventually agreed to do so, just so all the assholes would leave him alone. Zack's political aspirations up to this point had been non-existent. He had no opinions, didn't care about the issues, and had never voted in his life (not even for himself for president). Zack's campaign was mostly made up of him showing up in his military uniform and showing off his spitting skills.

Zack won the election easily, a fact that he was not aware of for several days due to his refusal to pay the postage fees for the congratulatory letter sent to him. With a bored sigh, Zack installed himself into the White House, letting his war horse, Whitney, graze the lawn and helping his wife, Margaret, install new locks on many of the rooms so she could be a crazy recluse in peace. Zack didn't really give two shits about government, and spent most his time avoiding doing his job, hiding from Congress and his cabinet, and sometimes locking himself up with Margaret for days at a time. Zack had no policies and no plans. About the only thing he did do as president was threaten to personally hang anyone who tried to secede.

Sixteen months into his presidency, Zack attended the opening ceremony of the phallus-like Washington Monument. It was a hot day, so Zack ate a whole bunch of cherries and drank a shit ton of milk. He enjoyed both so immensely that he gorged himself on milk and cherries for pretty much the entire day. He soon came down with a terrible tummy ache, which despite many attempts, could not be cured by spitting chewing tobacco long distances, resulting in his death. Historians agree that this was by far the most interesting part of Zack's presidency.

#13 Millard Fillmore
(1850-1853)
Number Thirteen Is Bad Luck

Mill Fill looked like a tuskless walrus shoved into a suit. Granted, he was an immaculately dressed tuskless walrus in a well cut dark suit, but a walrus nonetheless. Queen Victoria once claimed that Mill Fill was the handsomest man she had ever seen, which does not speak well for Queen Victoria, or the British people as a whole. Mill Fill was a sad sack who lived a life where nothing ever went right. It started from the beginning when he was born into abject poverty, living in a log cabin, and unable to go to school because he had to help out on the family farm. Considered bad luck by his family for some reason, his father gave him away, first to a cloth maker, and then to the owner of a textile mill. Both beat him, a lot.

Not enjoying life, Mill Fill decided to better himself. First, he taught himself how to read and write, and then he went to law school. There, he met and married Abigail Powers, who was not only two years his senior, but also his teacher. Some people just find learning that sexy. Mill Fill soon after moved into politics, joining the Anti-Mason party, which believed the Free Masons were plotting to take over the world. Yes, that was a real political party. Worried that people might think of him as an idiot, but not for the Anti-Mason thing, Mill Fill started carrying around a dictionary to prove how smart he was. Dictionary in hand, he would force himself into conversations so he could show off his new vocabulary words. In 1848, despite no one outside of upstate New York having any idea who he was, and the people who did know him not really liking him, Mill Fill was elected Vice President.

During his time as Vice President, Mill Fill wasn't even allowed to talk to President Zack because Zack couldn't stand to be around him. When Zack suddenly died, Mill Fill became president. He offered to give an inauguration speech, but everyone pretty much agreed that he totally didn't need to do that. Mill Fill's presidency was largely spent pissing off everyone he possibly could by finding compromises that never seemed to work out. When the election of 1852 came around, his party didn't even nominate him, instead going with another elderly war hero, General Winfield Scott, because though that strategy had never worked, it was still considered a better option than Mill Fill. About the only success he did have as president was installing the first running water bathtub in the White House.

Soon after leaving the presidency, Mill Fill's wife and daughter both died. Heartbroken, Mill Fill did the most logical thing and took an extravagant European vacation. The trip must not have gone well, because when he got back he joined the Know Nothing Party, which was super anti-immigrant. With his new racist friends, he ran for president again in 1856, but failed miserably. Nearly broke, Mill Fill married a half crazy wealthy widow named Caroline McIntosh, who wisely forced him to sign a prenup. Largely hated for the rest of his life, Mill Fill died of a sudden stroke while being fed some soup. His last words were, "the nutrition is palatable."

#14 Franklin Pierce
(1853-1857)
Drunk And Handsome

Frankie had a head of beautiful curly hair, which as he got older, turned into the most impressive comb over in presidential history. Frankie was born in a log cabin and spent much of his childhood learning how to be a depressed alcoholic from his mother. In college, Frankie studied law. He also hung out with the likes of Henry Longfellow and Nathaniel Hawthorne, two literary fellows. Together they spent their time being presumptuous 19th century hipster douche-bags. Questioning why they were even going to college, when you know, the whole world was such bullshit and all. After college Frankie married Jane Appleton, a minister's daughter who hated alcohol and despised politics. Soon after Frankie became an alcoholic and ran for Congress.

Frankie was the youngest Congressman of his era. He was considered dashing and handsome, though Queen Victoria with her apparent walrus fetish probably didn't agree. Frankie soon grew tired of politics, and convinced President Pokey, who had recently declared war on Mexico, to make him a general, despite his total lack of military experience. During the war, Frankie was badly wounded when he heroically fell off his horse, which is just something that alcoholics do from time to time. In 1852, he ran for president against the famous war hero General Winfield Scott, also known as Old Fuss and Feathers, a man so fat he looked as if he might die at any moment or be seduced by the Queen. Despite having the less than charming nickname of "The Hero of Many a Well Fought Bottle", Frankie won the general election by a landslide. This was probably due to the fact that the American people were pretty fed up with old dying generals with funny nicknames.

Frankie's presidency did not start out on a good note. Just a few short days before his inauguration his son was decapitated by a terrible train accident right in front of Frankie and his wife. Frankie just increased his drinking, but his wife, already a little unhinged, became a hermit. Luckily, President Zack had already installed locks in the White House for his own crazy wife, so it was an easy transition. At his inauguration ceremony, Frankie refused to use a bible for his oath of office, instead demanding to use a book of law. His popularity quickly soured when people realized that he had no leadership skills and was easily manipulated by asshats. Frankie's greatest achievements included supporting slavery, plotting to invade Cuba (but being too chicken to try it), and drunkenly running over an old lady with his carriage, a crime he got away with because he was the mother fucking president. When the election of 1856 rolled around, his own party refused to re-nominate him.

After leaving the presidency, Frankie took an extended vacation to Europe and the Bahamas, happily drinking away his troubles while his wife died of tuberculosis. During the Civil War, despite living in New Hampshire, Frankie supported the Confederacy and publicly called Abe Lincoln an asshole, a stance that wasn't all that popular at the time. In the end, Frankie's alcoholism caught up with him and he died of liver failure. At his funeral, everyone remarked on how good his hair looked.

#15 James Buchanan
(1857-1861)
Miss Nancy

Ten Spot, nicknamed Ten Cent Jimmy by his opponents, was born in a log cabin, which apparently was a requirement to be president in the mid-nineteenth century. Ten Spot was a weird dude, described as an effeminate, winking, fidgeting, little busy body. The winking was probably a little off-putting given that he had one green eye and one brown eye. Ten Spot did not have a happy childhood. His best friend growing up was his pet parrot Betsy Ross, who he probably taught how to say, "James is the coolest." Ten Spot went to law school, but quit for a short period to fight in the War of 1812, where he lost his middle finger. Soon after, he went into politics. Ten Spot never got married. He did court a woman named Anne Coleman for a while, but she broke off the engagement and killed herself shortly after, which seemed like a pretty good excuse for Ten Spot to stay a bachelor.

Ten Spot was gay. While he never climbed his way to the top of the Washington Monument and officially proclaimed it or anything, he didn't do a whole lot to hide it either. Ten Spot lived for ten years with fellow Congressman William Rufus King. People, being the assholes that they have always been, often referred to the pair as Mr. and Mrs. Buchanan, the Siamese Twins, or Miss Nancy and Aunt Fancy. Those ten years were probably the only happy years in Ten Spot's entire life. When King died, Ten Spot lamented that though he courted other men, he'd never find another one like King.

In 1856, Ten Spot was elected president because he had spent the past several years in England, and hence, was the politician who had the fewest enemies. At the time, the U.S. was in a crisis with states threatening to secede over the slavery issue. Instead of dealing with that, Ten Spot spent most of his time going to church, raising pygmy goats at the White House, and getting ridiculously drunk. Oh yeah, probably should have mentioned that earlier. Ten Spot was a huge alcoholic. He once stated that Russians were a bunch of pussies when it came to drinking. Unsurprisingly, getting black out drunk did little to settle the slavery issue, and by the end of his term seven states had seceded from the Union. Ten Spot reacted by declaring that seceding was technically illegal, but that so was going to war prevent it. He then pretty much spent the rest of his presidency twiddling his thumbs.

Ten Spot was mysteriously not re-nominated in 1860, and when Honest Abe became president, he pretty much handed over the keys to the White house and said good luck with that shit. In retirement, Ten Spot supported the fighting of the Civil War, which apparently in his mind was no longer illegal, and spent his time writing a memoir on why he wasn't a total fuck up. His detractors claimed his writing was just as poor as his presidency. In the end, Ten Spot caught a bad cold and died of respiratory failure, which is a fancy medical term meaning he quit breathing, which often happens when one dies.

#16 Abraham Lincoln
(1861-1865)
The Frankenstein Of Freedom

Many claim Abe was born in a log cabin. In reality he was cobbled together by Dr. Frankenstein. The man was a giant ugly dude. We're talking so ugly that a little girl wrote him a letter suggesting that he grow a beard to hide his ugly face, and instead of getting angry, he admitted that she might just have a point. When Abe was a child he was kicked in the head by a horse and lay half dead for a week. Soon after, his mother died after drinking some poisoned milk. Hating his father, Abe spent his youth wandering from town to town, challenging people to wrestling contests which he won easily thanks to his great height and ridiculously long limbs. Abe was awkward and shy around women, but managed to convince one named Mary Todd to marry him. However, Abe broke off the engagement when he figured out that Mary was crazy, but reconsidered when he remembered that he was no prize himself. On the day of their marriage, Abe declared that he felt like he was going to hell.

Abe didn't really know what to do with himself. Wrestling wasn't paying the bills and he only had eighteen months of formal education under his belt. He tried being a bar owner (despite that fact that he did not drink), postmaster, and ferry operator. Abe then read some law books and declared himself a lawyer, something that you could apparently do back then. Abe then went into politics, and though he wasn't very good at it, he became renowned for his amazing speeches, which were apparently so enthralling that people forgot to write most of them down. His nemesis in the political field was Stephen Douglas, a very short man who had coincidentally been his rival suitor for the hand of crazy ass Mary Todd. It was during this period that Abe started wearing his signature stovepipe hat, which he used to hold his speeches, bills, and other important documents.

Abe was elected president in 1860 on the platform of fuck the South let's just free the slaves. This was not popular in the South, which formed its own country, creatively called the Confederacy, which was apparently named when its leaders looked up the word United in the thesaurus. The Civil War raged throughout Abe's presidency, a very stressful time that Abe dealt with by becoming extremely depressed, staying in bed for days at a time, and having fancy dinners of oysters with his cat, imaginatively named Tabby, who was allowed to sit at the table and was fed with a golden fork. Not to be out crazied, his wife forced him to attend séances to try and contact their dead children. Abe's depression became so bad that he refused to carry a pocket knife because he was afraid he might kill himself with it. Abe was re-elected in 1864, won the Civil War, and freed all the slaves, though only in the Confederacy.

One night, Abe had a dream of his own funeral, which understandably freaked him out. To try and relax he attended a comedy at the Ford Theater where famous actor John Wilkes Booth shot him in the head, which is comparable to Brad Pitt shooting the president today. Even in death, Abe had no luck. His wife, Mary, went even more insane, which is probably a fair response to having your husband's brains in your lap. She held weekly séances and was later committed to an insane asylum. A year after Abe died, a hardcore and drunk former Confederate assassinated his dog, who, it may not surprise you to learn, was named Fido. Eleven years after his death, a group of inept criminals tried to kidnap his dead body to hold it for ransom. After the plot was foiled, his remains were buried under ten feet of concrete.

#17 Andrew Johnson
(1865-1869)
A Hillbilly Goes To Washington

Andy was born in a log cabin (seriously, did they not have normal houses back then?) to illiterate hillbilly parents. Andy's parents, distrustful of book learning, never sent Andy to school. Instead, they let him run around like a wild animal, guzzling moonshine, and in general acting like nineteenth century white trash. When his parents ran low on cash, they sold him to a tailor, who taught Andy the trade, and also occasionally beat him. Tiring of such a life, Andy ran away and set up his own tailor shop. At age 18, Andy married a 17 year old girl named Eliza McCardle. Eliza was sickly and shy, but also a well educated young woman. Her parents were undeniably disappointed by the fact that the apple of their eye had married an illiterate redneck, but Eliza saw potential in her chosen husband and proceeded to polish the turd that he was, teaching him reading, writing, and basic math.

With his newfound brains, Andy launched a political career, eventually working his way up to U.S. Senator by the time the Civil War broke out. When all the other southern senators left to join the Confederacy, Andy stayed in Washington DC, pretending that he was still supposed to be there. In 1864, Andy was elected Abe's Vice President. Andy celebrated by getting extremely drunk the day of his inauguration, slurring and mumbling his way through his partially coherent speech. Horribly embarrassed, Andy decided that it would probably be best for everybody if he just skipped town without telling anyone. However, before he could, President Abe got shot in the head. Andy was supposed to get shot too, but luckily his assassin was just as inept as he was, getting too drunk to carry out the deed.

Andy didn't really want to be president and really wasn't all that popular. He was known for being overly blunt, tactless, cold, stubborn, and impatient. Andy spent much of his presidency sewing his own suits (he was a tailor after all), hanging out with his invalid wife who was too sick to get out of bed, caring for a family of white mice he found in the White House, and buying a huge tract of empty land called Alaska. He also kept himself busy vetoing bills that would have given more rights to African-Americans, earning himself the nickname Sir Veto. Congress, tiring of his shit, tried to impeach him, but failed by a single vote. When the next election rolled around, Andy was not re-nominated to run again. Andy spent the last few months of his presidency throwing himself a lavish 60th birthday party attended by hundreds of children, which is impossible to write about in a way that does not make it sound creepy as hell.

Andy was decidedly bitter about his White House experience, and spent his retirement stewing over strange revenge plots and insisting to anyone who would listen that he really wasn't that bad of a guy. Seven years after leaving the White House, thanks to the support of the important illiterate hillbilly voting bloc, Andy was elected to the U.S. Senate again. The victory made him so happy that he had a stroke and died.

#18 Ulysses S. Grant
(1869-1877)
More Cigar Than Man

Useless, a nickname given to him by his parents, was born, unlike many of his predecessors, in an actual house to upper middle class parents. His given name was Hiram, but while applying to join the West Point military academy the government screwed up his application form, changing his name to Ulysses. The government refused to rectify the mistake and gave Useless the option of either changing his name or not attending West Point. Useless chose the former. Useless was a pretty shitty student at West Point, but was the best in his class at riding horses so was made an officer. Being a bit of a douche, Useless decided that he wanted to nail his West Point roommate's hot sister, Julia Boggs Dent, so he hounded her constantly until she agreed to marry him.

During the Mexican War, Useless made a name for himself by crazily riding his horse at people and killing them. After the war, he was kicked out of the Army for being a drunk. Useless tried his hand at being a real estate agent, but failed, forcing him to switch careers to selling firewood on street corners and mooching money off of his relatives. When the Civil War broke out, the Army decided they could ignore things like extreme alcoholism, and Useless was welcomed back into the military. He soon after earned the rank of general after perfecting the winning strategy of sending wave after wave of men against enemy lines until the defenders ran out of bullets. Useless spent the entire war in a drunken haze, riding half broke horses, dressing like a hobo, getting sick at the sight of blood (a rare steak would make him nauseous), and making sure absolutely nobody ever saw him naked (including his wife). Despite having no political experience, a fact he regularly mentioned to anyone who would listen, he was elected president in 1868.

Useless was the youngest president up to that point in time, and it showed. Instead of appointing people who actually knew what they were doing to government positions, he instead appointed his friends, who all turned out to be corrupt assholes who were more interested in stealing than actually doing their jobs. Despite this, Useless was re-elected president in 1872 after his opponent politely bowed out of the race by dying. As president, Useless largely quit drinking to make sure his mind remained clear. Instead, he took to eating, yes eating, not smoking, twenty cigars a day. This resulted in Useless having a constant sore throat which his old timey doctors treated with cocaine, which Useless then became mysteriously addicted to. High as a kite, Useless would ride his horse at full tilt down the streets of Washington DC, which once earned him a speeding ticket when a policeman failed to recognize him as the president.

After his presidency, Useless went on an around the world tour. Soon after, for some reason, he went completely broke. In need of money, Useless first tried to run for president again, but failed because beards were back in fashion and his just wasn't impressive enough. He then wrote his memoirs, which despite not including vampires or lurid sex scenes, were considered to be pretty good. Useless died of throat cancer, which was probably totally unrelated to his tobacco chomping ways. A humble man, he was buried in the largest mausoleum in North America.

#19 Rutherford B. Hayes
(1877-1881)
Mr. Excitement Himself

Granny (so called because he didn't drink, smoke, or gamble) was probably the nicest, but most boring, man to ever be president. When Granny's mother told his father that she was pregnant, his father became so happy that he fell over and died. His mother, who never remarried, raised Granny on her own, teaching him to avoid excitement at all costs. Granny spent most of his time studying, because it was what his mother told him to do. This resulted in him graduating from Harvard and becoming a lawyer. As a lawyer, Granny became famous for perfecting the insanity defense, by pointing out that anyone who would hire him as a lawyer had to be a little crazy. When the Mexican War broke out, Granny considered joining the Army, but decided to instead visit a friend in New England.

Granny married Lucy Webb, a well-educated woman, pretty much just because his mother told him to. Are you sensing a pattern here? Soon after the Civil War broke out, Granny, ignoring his mother's advice for the first time ever, joined the Army and became a Major General. Granny probably should have listened to his mother, as he was shot in five different battles and was erroneously listed as dead for a period of time, which led to a great amount of difficulty in getting himself declared alive again. After the war, Granny went into politics, where he was successful because he was a nice man with an epic beard. In 1876, he ran for president on the very liberal idea that pretty much everybody was the same regardless of race. The 1876 election was very contentious, with lots of back room deals and voter intimidation and fraud. In the end, a compromise was made. Granny got to be president, but in return the South got to go back to being blatant racists. This earned Granny the nicknames His Fraudulency and Rutherfraud. Both of which really hurt his feelings.

Granny was given his oath of office in secret because it was worried that his opponents would try to derail his inauguration by booing or something. His opponents did try to impeach him, but failed because his supporters just didn't show up to the meeting. Lacking a quorum, the vote could not take place. Upon entering the White House, Granny banned drinking, smoking, dancing, and playing cards. When people complained, Granny told them it was because of his wife, so people started calling her Lemonade Lucy. To try and make up for the lack of fun, Granny started leading the singing of gospel hymns every morning, had a telephone installed at the White House (a device he claimed would never catch on), and imported the first Siamese cat into America (which he creatively named Siam). Having little else to do, Granny spent the last 70 days of his presidency touring the West Coast and boring the hell out of the people there.

No one wanted Granny to run for a second term, so he told everyone that he didn't believe in second terms and didn't run. After his presidency, he continued his legacy of being a dull nice man by spending his time supporting educational foundations and pushing for prison reform. In one last attempt to be interesting, he died of a heart attack and was buried with his wife and his favorite horse, Old Whitey. The Siamese cat was not buried with them, because that would have just been silly.

#20 James A. Garfield
(1881)
Not A Cat

Boatman Jim's dad moved out to the frontier to marry a beautiful woman. When he discovered that the woman was already married, he said what the hell and married her sister as a consolation prize. This very romantic union produced Boatman Jim, who they named after his dead older brother, because why waste a perfectly good name. While Boatman Jim was still a baby, his dad died, leaving the family to live in terrible poverty in a log cabin. They were pretty much nineteenth century trailer trash. The family couldn't even afford shoes. This led to Boatman Jim being constantly made fun of by the other children, something he dealt with by keeping his nose buried in a book while his doting mother told him that all those mean kids were just jealous of how cool he was.

While still quite young, Boatman Jim left home and got himself a job on a canal boat, earning the worst presidential nickname ever. Deciding that boating sucked ass, he went to college, earning money to pay for it by working as a janitor and a bell ringer. After graduating, Boatman Jim worked as a teacher, lawyer, and preacher. It was during his tenure as a teacher that he met his one true love, Lucretia Rudolph, who also happened to be one of his students. Boatman Jim fought in the Civil War for a little while, but later quit to go into politicking. In 1880, his party couldn't agree on who should run for president, so they instead just pointed randomly into the crowd and decided Boatman Jim should do it. Boatman Jim, not big on travelling, took the novel campaign approach of just sitting on the front porch of his dilapidated house and waiting for people to come up and ask him questions. Somehow, this worked, and he won the election.

Even as president, Boatman Jim was poor as hell. He even had to borrow a horse and carriage from former President Granny to get around. Boatman Jim spent most of his presidency impressing visitors by writing in Greek with one hand while simultaneously writing in Latin with the other, declaring a national holiday so people could go decorate Civil War graves, and juggling bowling pins to build his manly physique. Like many people with rock hard bodies, Boatman Jim had a stalker. During the election, one Charlie Guiteau, who was all sorts of crazy, had ranted and raved in the streets about how Boatman Jim should be president. Mr. Guiteau felt that this unasked for service had earned him a government job. When he was not given a government job, he bought a gun that he thought would look good in a museum one day and used it to shoot Boatman Jim.

The shooting of Boatman Jim left the old timey doctors of the time with a perplexing medical case because they were unable to find the bullet lodged in his spine. They tried to use an old timey metal detector to find the bullet, but it kept getting false positives because of the metal springs in the mattress. This didn't stop the doctors from cutting numerous holes into Boatman Jim and probing the holes with their dirty fingers. After eighty days of these shenanigans, Boatman Jim very reasonably died of blood poisoning. The doctors than cut out his spine (to finally find that pesky bullet) and put it on display in a museum.

#21 Chester A. Arthur
(1881-1885)
I Am The Walrus

The Walrus was named after the doctor who oversaw his birth, who also happened to be a good friend of his father. The Walrus's father was a Canadian preacher, which is probably why he never thought to question why his wife would insist they name their brand new baby after a man who was always hanging out around his house. The Walrus, thanks to his middle class upbringing, attended university, where he studied law, beat up supporters of President Pokey, and threw the school bell into Lake Erie. After graduating he moved to New York City where he worked as a lawyer, defending African-American's civil rights. However, this didn't pay the bills, so he got himself appointed to a government position at the Port of New York, where he made himself rich on bribes and graft.

The Walrus had a reputation for being a snappy dresser (ill-gotten money has its perks). He was often called Elegant Arthur, The Gentleman Boss, Prince Arthur, and the Dude President. When the Walrus fought in the Civil War, he used his connections to make sure he got a job behind the front lines where his uniform could stay in immaculate condition. His inscrutable dress sense undoubtedly won him the hand of his wife, Ellen Herndon, who wasn't so bad herself on the looks scale. Of course, the Walrus's fat wallet full of bribe money probably didn't hurt either. The Walrus's misdeeds ended up catching up with him, and he was fired from his job for corruption. This was shortly followed by his election to the Vice Presidency. When President Boatman Jim was assassinated in 1881, the Walrus became president, an event that made his wife so happy, that she promptly expired.

The start of the Walrus's presidency was contentious. First, he had to take the oath of office twice, because apparently it has to be done by a federal official, not just some random friend. Second, people made all sorts of wild claims, like the Walrus had actually been born in Canada and that he had orchestrated the assassination of Boatman Jim. Undeterred, the Walrus, a man of luxury, refused to move into the White House until it was redecorated up to his extravagant tastes. To pay for the renovation, he auctioned off all of the historical items already in it. Most of the Walrus's presidency was spent trying to decide which one of his eighty pairs of pants he should wear, changing his outfit three or four times a day, hosting lavish parties, going to night clubs, and just strolling around the streets of Washington DC until three in the god damn morning.

While still president, the Walrus discovered he had a deadly kidney disease. Keeping it hidden from the public, he traveled to Yellowstone to see if drinking boiling sulfur water would prolong his life, or perhaps he was actually just looking for the entrance to hell so he could make a deal with the devil. Whatever the reason, his health continued to deteriorate and he did not run for a second term. The day he left office, four women asked him to marry them. Eighteen months later he died. The last thing the Walrus did was burn all of his personal and official papers, which is about the worst way to disprove conspiracies that you had your predecessor assassinated.

#22 Grover Cleveland
(1885-1889)
A Fat Pervy Bastard

Uncle Jumbo, so called because he was a big fat bastard, was the son of a middle class Presbyterian minister. His given name was Steven, but due to mean kids calling him Big Steven Cleveland, he changed it to Grover, which was definitely a much cooler name at the time. The mean kids then changed his nickname to Uncle Jumbo. Uncle Jumbo was a cheeky youth, often playing pranks on his friends and neighbors, as if he was some kind of chubby Dennis the Menace. After putting himself through college he worked for a time as a teacher for the blind, and then a lawyer. Not a lawyer for the blind, just a regular lawyer. When the Civil War broke out, Uncle Jumbo got drafted, but got out of having to fight by paying a Polish immigrant to take his place. He then went on to become a sheriff for a time, where he gained a reputation for hanging numerous people and getting drunk in saloons.

Growing bored of drunken executions, Uncle Jumbo went back to lawyering, but soon found himself in a dilly of a pickle. Possibly as some kind of bizarre team building exercise, all the partners in his law firm had been sleeping with the same woman. When the woman became pregnant, Uncle Jumbo, being the only bachelor, bit the bullet and started paying child support. This situation became more difficult as Uncle Jumbo began getting into politics, but he solved it by having the woman committed to an insane asylum and putting the baby up for adoption. In 1884, Uncle Jumbo was chosen to run for president because all the other possible candidates were somehow bigger jackasses then he was. Unfortunately, the question of his possibly illegitimate child came up again. Where most politicians would have lied, Uncle Jumbo took the unorthodox approach of just shrugging his shoulders and admitting that the baby might have been his, but he really wasn't all that sure. And while this didn't exactly set a precedent in truth telling for future candidates, he did win the election.

The first thing Uncle Jumbo did after becoming president was marry a college-aged woman twenty-seven years his junior named Frances Folsom. Frances was the daughter of one of Uncle Jumbo's best friends. Uncle Jumbo had doted on the child since the day she born, bouncing her on his knee and buying her numerous gifts. When she was eleven, her father died, so he took it upon himself to supervise her upbringing. Looking back at all of this today, the creepiest part wasn't the fact that Uncle Jumbo apparently groomed Frances from a young age to be his wife, but that pretty much the whole country was okay with it. Uncle Jumbo did other things during his presidency, such as vetoing more bills than all his predecessors combined, but holy shit, the man was basically Woody Allen if Woody Allen had somehow gotten himself elected president and gained 130 pounds.

Uncle Jumbo lost his bid for re-election in 1888, but not for reasons related to the fact that he was creepy as fuck. As Uncle Jumbo left the White House, his almost child bride swore they would be back in four years.

#23 Benjamin Harrison
(1889-1893)
The Human Iceberg

Little Ben, also called the Human Iceberg for his stiff and formal manner when dealing with people, was the grandson of President Tippy. Born on the family farm, Little Ben spent his youth happily hunting and fishing. However, as he got older, he apparently turned into a fastidious little bitch. Worried about infection, Little Ben started wearing leather gloves all the time, earning himself the nickname Kid Gloves. As if being a germaphobe wasn't bad enough, when Little Ben went to college, he gained a reputation as a brown-noser. He was such a suck up that he married Lavinia Scott, the daughter of one of his most prominent professors.

After graduating from university, Little Ben went to work as a lawyer. When the Civil War broke out, he joined the Army, but spent most of his time guarding railroads. As the war came to a close, his unit was sent into Georgia where Little Ben went a little nuts, burning and looting like some kind of half madman, half human wrecking ball. Though to be totally fair, everyone in Georgia was doing basically the same thing at the time. After the war, Little Ben decided to get into politics, but despite running numerous times, no one would vote for him. This made Little Ben super mopey, so mopey that one of his friends finally got him appointed as a Senator just so he'd quit being such a whiney little bitch. In 1888, Little Ben was nominated to run for president because the other two possible people were total ass hats. Little Ben won, mostly because at the time having an epic beard was still considered enough of a qualification to be president.

It rained the day of Little Ben's inauguration, bringing back bad memories of President Tippy's demise, but luckily, former president Uncle Jumbo agreed to hold an umbrella over Little Ben while he made his speech. Little Ben loved making speeches. Once during his presidency, he made 140 different ones in a single month. All of them were boring as hell. Little Ben also had a thing for goats. He kept several goats with him at the White House, and gave all of his grandchildren goats for their birthdays. Little Ben was the first president to have electricity installed in the White House. However, both he and his wife were afraid of getting electrocuted and refused to touch the switches. This led to many an awkward night where they were forced to sleep with the lights on. Worried about his chances for re-election in 1892, Little Ben brought six new states into the Union to better his chances. This strategy proved pointless since his wife got sick, and instead of campaigning, he stayed at her side until she died.

After his presidency, Little Ben went back to being a lawyer. He also got himself a hot new young wife, 25 years his junior, named Mary Scott Dimmick, who just so happened to also be his wife's sister's daughter, which is a roundabout way of saying he married his niece. For some weird reason his kids weren't happy about their father taking their cousin as his bride, and most of them never talked to him again. Little Ben died of pneumonia after getting a bad case of the flu, probably caught because he touched something while not wearing his god damn gloves.

#24 Grover Cleveland
(1893-1897)
The Return of The Fat Man

The day Uncle Jumbo got booted out of the White House, his almost child bride declared that they would be back in four years. Uncle Jumbo spent those years making babies, obsessively fishing, drinking copious amounts of booze, and smoking numerous cigars. He also went back to lawyering, but this was mostly so he could have an office in which he could drink and smoke in peace. The intervening years were a Rocky training montage, only with Uncle Jumbo getting fatter and less fit. In 1892, the Uncle Jumbo versus Little Ben rematch finally took place. The 1888 election had been a down and dirty grudge match, and many people expected 1892 to be one for the ages. Those people were disappointed. Uncle Jumbo won by a landslide thanks to his competitor being too busy taking care of his dying wife to have time to campaign.

Uncle Jumbo, with the haughty (and heavy) footsteps of a vindicated man, victoriously returned to the White House, and was promptly blindsided by the collapse of the American economy. Uncle Jumbo attempted to solve the problem by begging rich people for money, having the Army shoot railroad strikers, and even doing absolutely nothing. When none of these solutions worked, Uncle Jumbo tried developing a cancerous tumor in his mouth. The tumor didn't fix the economy, but it did force Uncle Jumbo to have a secret surgery on a friend's yacht in the middle of the night. The media of course grew curious about all of the secretive goings on. When they asked Uncle Jumbo why part of his jaw was suddenly missing, he told them that they were mistaken and that was what his face had always looked like. It being a very different time, people took him at his word, and the matter was dropped.

The shitty economy took its toll on Uncle Jumbo's presidency. He was not nominated to run again in 1896, and so, his husky tail back between his legs, he went back into retirement. Uncle Jumbo spent his second retirement much like the first; fishing and drinking himself stupid. However, instead of making babies, he started a new hobby of writing articles for women's magazines advising that sensible and respectable women did not want the right to vote. Uncle Jumbo died of a heart attack, probably brought on by the fact that he was a big fat bastard. His wife soon after remarried an archeologist who was closer to her own age and weight bracket.

#25 William McKinley
(1897-1901)
The Industrialist's Stooge

Wobbly Willy, so called because of his cautious and indecisive nature, was born to a wealthy upper crust family. His father, Willy Senior, owned numerous foundries. Wobbly Willy was originally a junior, but abandoned the moniker the day his father died in what amounted to an old timey fuck you dad. Like many rich kids, Wobbly had the opportunity to attend the finest schools, an opportunity, which like many rich kids, he squandered. After just a year at university, he returned home, claiming all the learning was making him sick and depressed. School was no fun, Wobbly enjoyed spending his family's money a lot more. When the Civil War broke out, Wobbly joined the Army and got put under the command of the future President Granny. Wobbly, a husky lad, spent most of the war working as a clerk.

After the war, Wobbly returned home to discover that his family had gone broke. Robbed of his chosen lifestyle as a lay about, Wobbly went back to university and became a lawyer. He then married Ida Saxton, who though being best described as sickly and a little strange, did come from an extremely rich family. This matrimonial union opened up a whole new world for Wobbly, who started rubbing shoulders with millionaires. These millionaires decided that Wobbly would be the perfect puppet for their interests. Backed by their money, Wobbly entered politics, always wearing a red carnation in his lapel for luck. In 1896 he was elected president, boosted by the most expensive political campaign in history up to that time.

The early years of Wobbly's presidency were mostly spent teaching his parrot, named Washington Post, to whistle the tune to Yankee Doodle Dandy, and taking care of his sickly wife. The couple had two children who both died young, and the strain had resulted in her developing epilepsy. She'd often have seizures in public, and Wobbly, being a doting husband, would cover her face with a handkerchief and carry on as though nothing strange was happening. By the time Wobbly became president, her mind had started to go too. She refused to move into the White House until everything yellow was removed, including the flowers, and mostly spent her time crocheting thousands of slippers. Wobbly's later presidency was mostly spent beating up on weaker countries and stealing their toys, a.k.a. their overseas territories. This proved quite popular, and he easily won re-election in 1900.

Wobbly loved people, and spent a lot of time shaking as many hands as possible. It was while at one of the palm pumping exhibitions that he became the first president to ride in an automobile. Unfortunately, this automobile was an ambulance. Seconds after giving his lucky red carnation to a little girl, a crazy anarchist shot him twice in the gut for reasons that can best be described as unhinged. Doctors were unable to find one of the bullets because, as they put it, Wobbly was too fat. Eight days later he died of a nasty infection. Wobbly's wife did not attend his funeral, but instead stayed home and made more slippers.

#26 Theodore Roosevelt
(1901-1909)
Nothing But Teeth And Testicles

Teedie, who tried to give himself the nickname Colonel, was born into a wealthy family. A sickly child, he was diagnosed with asthma, a condition which his old timey doctors treated with cigars and whiskey. Fearing for his health, Teedie's parents kept him locked away and isolated in the family mansion for most of his childhood. Teedie spent most of his time reading books, being educated by private tutors, and shooting and then stuffing small animals like some kind of serial killer. While attending university, Teedie was told he had a weak heart. In response, he took up every sport possible, until he had no time for school and dropped out. This caught the eye of a lovely woman named Alice Hathaway Lee. They spent their honeymoon climbing the Matterhorn.

Teedie's life took a bad turn when both his mother and wife died on the same day. To grieve, Teedie moved out west, became a cowboy, and got in fights with random strangers. His bereavement done, he returned to the East Coast, entered public service, and got himself a new wife, Edith Kermit Carow. While serving as the Assistant Secretary of the Navy, he got bored, lied on some memos, and started a war with Spain. He then resigned, formed his own cavalry unit, joined the invasion of Cuba, and became a war hero. This new war hero status led to him getting elected Vice President in 1900. When President Wobbly got shot in 1901, Teedie became the youngest president ever.

Teedie spent most of his presidency metaphorically, and angrily, waving his dick in people's faces. An avid outdoorsman, he spent most of his time taking strenuous hikes through local parks, blasting away at twigs with his revolver, and swimming naked in the Potomac River. Teedie was also an avid boxer, often challenging people to friendly bouts at the White House, until a lucky punch blinded him in one eye. He then took up jiu-jitsu. In 1904, Teedie was re-elected. His second term was full of just as much angry dick waving and nature humping. Somehow, Teedie won the Nobel Peace Prize, convincing Japan and Russia to sign a peace treaty by using the negotiation tactic of taking the delegates into the woods and showing them his revolver. Teedie celebrated his achievement by becoming the first president to fly in an airplane, probably waving his hat about and yelling the whole god damn time for the Wright Brothers to do a barrel roll. Growing bored, Teedie declined to run for president again in 1908.

After leaving the White House, Teedie went on an African safari where he pretty much shot every animal in existence, even some you've probably never heard of because they don't exist anymore. Returning home, he decided he wanted to be president again and ran as an independent in 1912. This move proved unpopular, and a crazy man shot him in the chest. Teedie, ignoring the blood covering his shirt, gave a ninety minute speech before going to the hospital. Teedie got over his loss by going to South America to find the source of a branch of the Amazon River, and probably shoot it. The entire expedition caught malaria, including Teedie, but by god, they found the source of that river nobody cared about. When World War I broke out, Teedie asked the government for permission to raise a personal army of 200,000 men to lead to France, a request that was denied for reasons of being insane. This angered Teedie, who then decided to run for president again. It was at this point that his weak heart, having enough of Teedie's special brand of crazy bullshit, gave out.

#27 William H. Taft
(1909-1913)
Rub A Dub Dub Fat Dude In A Tub

Let's just get it out of the way right now, Big Lub, also known as Big Bill and Big Chief, was a portly fellow. The guy weighed 330 pounds when he was president. He was a fat man, a fat kid, and probably a fat baby too. Born into an upper crust family, Big Lub spent his childhood going to fancy private schools and earning a reputation as a girthy intellectual. With the combination of fat and smart, you better believe the other kids teased the shit out of him. Big Lub though took it all in stride, and when he attended university, he joined the wrestling team, where his walrus-like stature allowed him to beat the crap out of all his opponents. Besides wrestling, Big Lub also enjoyed tennis, golf, and horseback riding, much to the chagrin of the horse. For a fat man, Big Lub was known as one hell of a dancer. It was probably his fancy dance steps, and maybe a bit of a fat fetish, which caught the eye of the woman who became his wife, Nellie Herron.

Following law school, Big Lub was appointed to several federal judicial posts. However, his wife, believing her husband was destined for big things (no pun intended), pushed him to accept a post as the Governor of the Philippines, which at the time was owned by the U.S. and going through a guerilla war which was the Vietnam of its day. Big Lub dealt with the war by gaining more weight, an impressive feat considering he also contracted dengue fever. Returning to the U.S., Big Lub became best buds with President Teedie, who decided that Big Lub would make a perfect president. Big Lub didn't want to be president, he wanted to be Chief Justice of the Supreme Court (which is weird given by this point he had already turned down the position three times), but the strong personalities of Nellie and Teedie won the day. Big Lub was elected president in 1908 thanks to the voters being scared of Teedie's revolver and Nellie's death stare. Nellie was so overcome with happiness that she died of a stroke soon after.

Big Lub spent most of his presidency eating pounds of almonds, farting, attending baseball games, and falling asleep during meetings (which was hard to hide given he was a terrible snorer). The presidency was not a happy time for Big Lub. Though a jolly fat man with an infectious chuckle, he really didn't know how to relate to people and was quite lonely. His depression led to him getting even fatter. Things hit a low when he got stuck in the White House bathtub and six aides had to pry him out using pounds of butter for lubricant. A new tub was shortly after installed, one big enough to fit four men. Big Lub was also the first president to own an automobile, probably to save the poor horses the strain of carting his fat ass around. By the end of his presidency, Big Lub was a wreck, openly crying on several occasions. When the 1912 election rolled around, his former best friend, Teedie, pissed that Big Lub was not doing exactly as he had been told, ran against Big Lub, splitting the vote. Big Lub came in a distant third.

Out of the White House, Big Lub's life improved dramatically. He dropped 75 pounds, started teaching, and spent most of his time writing letters railing against the supporters of prohibition. Big Lub did his best to forget that he had ever been president. Later in life he finally obtained his dream, becoming the Chief Justice of the Supreme Court. As he got older, Big Lub became very forgetful, even forgetting the presidential oath of office while administering it, and started hallucinating. In the end, Big Lub died of cardiovascular disease, because while he had lost some weight, he was still an extremely fat man.

#28 Woodrow Wilson
(1913-1921)
An American Vegetable

Tommy, yeah that's right, his actual name was Tommy, was born and raised in the Confederacy by a racist slave owning minister. Not trusting the Yankee schools at the end of the Civil War, Tommy's father decided that it was best for his young son, a sickly boy, to be homeschooled, of which the family did a bang up job, Tommy not learning to read until age 10. Despite his beginnings as an illiterate idiot, Tommy went to university. It was here that he changed his name to Woodrow because he thought it sounded cooler and would get him more chicks. It was a very different time. With his cool new name, Tommy managed to attract the attention of a young woman named Ellen Louise Axson, who gave up a promising art career to be with him. They got engaged, but unfortunately the wedding was delayed by her father going insane and killing himself, which was hopefully unrelated to the coming nuptials.

Tommy really enjoyed going to university. He enjoyed it so much he stayed until he had a PhD in Political Science. Like most people with a degree in Political Science, Tommy then got a job as a university professor. This led to him becoming a university president, a promotion he celebrated by having a stroke and going blind in one eye. The stroke also turned him from a pretty nice guy to an impatient and intolerant asshole. So he pretty much had a movie villain back story at this point. To recover from his stroke, Tommy went to Bermuda and had an affair. For some reason, this affair convinced Tommy that since he had spent his career writing about politics, he might as well put up or shut up. He entered politics and two years later, in 1912, got himself elected president thanks to former best friends Big Lub and Teedie splitting his opposition.

There were two things that Tommy hated, big business and black people. He promoted worker rights, but also promoted racist policies that strengthened segregation. When he wasn't busy being a racist dick, he spent most of his time driving his car around aimlessly for no damn good reason and disappointing visitors to the White House by serving grape juice instead of wine. It was during this time that his wife died, an event Tommy mourned by marrying a woman named Edith Galt. In 1916, Tommy won a second term by promising to keep the U.S. out of World War I, a promise he soon broke. To fight the war, he created an income tax, pretty much nationalized the country's industry, and made it illegal to bad mouth the government. Tommy spent the remainder of his presidency going slowly insane, making irrational decisions, and throwing temper tantrums. This behavior culminated in him having a second stroke, which left him mostly paralyzed and blind. His wife, Edith, seizing a golden opportunity, refused to let anyone see Tommy, becoming the sole means of communication between him and the outside world. It was at this time that Tommy mysteriously switched his stance on woman's suffrage, which led to women getting the right to vote.

Tommy didn't do much after leaving the presidency, probably because he was pretty much a vegetable by that time. He continued to mentally degrade as time went on, returning to the blithering idiot that he was when he was a child. About his only entertainment was his wife taking him out on daily automobile rides so people could see him drooling on himself. Soon after leaving the White House, Tommy had a third stroke, which finally did him in.

#29 Warren G. Harding
(1921-1923)
Possibly Your Real Great Grandfather

I want you to look at Winnie's picture. That is the look Winnie gave your great grandmother right before he took her to pound town. Winnie was born into a middle class family and had an uninteresting childhood. As an adult, he purchased and ran a local newspaper. Soon after buying his newspaper he married Florence Mabel King. Florence was a divorcee, Winnie's sister's piano teacher, and coincidentally the daughter of Winnie's rival in the local newspaper biz, because there is no better way to get under your rival's skin quite like copulating with his daughter. Florence really didn't want to marry Winnie, but he hounded her until she finally agreed just so he'd leave her alone. Winnie enjoyed the married life, mostly because it was a great way to meet women. He slept with all of his wife's friends, even having one affair for over a decade. He got away with it because he was considered handsome, charming, and had unusually large feet.

Winnie was quite content with his life of running a newspaper, screwing anything that moved, and writing erotic love letters to his various mistresses in which he nicknamed his penis Jerry, which was probably short for something. However, his wife wanted more. She pushed Winnie to enter politics, where he slowly worked his way up to Senator. When the 1920 presidential election came around, his party couldn't agree on a candidate, so they compromised by choosing Winnie, an interesting choice given that he had probably slept with all of their wives. Winnie's campaign largely involved openly declaring that he would make a terrible president, bribing his former mistresses so they'd keep their mouths shut, and trying to hide the fact he had recently had a love child with his good friend's 23 year old daughter. Though in his defense, the young woman had stalked him for years, so Winnie probably figured she had earned it. Somehow, none of these shenanigans got into the papers, and Winnie was elected president. Coincidentally, this was the first election women were allowed to vote.

Winnie really had no interest in being president. He spent most his time drinking whiskey (even though this was during the time of prohibition), playing poker with his ass hat friends (all of whom were given cushy government jobs), introducing the women of DC to Jerry, and writing increasingly erotic love letters (the man had a talent). Winnie himself declared several times that he was unfit to be president, but people just laughed and thought he was joking. His wife, Florence, understandably became increasingly unhinged and got into astrology and homeopathic medicine. Unsurprisingly, all of Winnie's poker buddies turned out to be corrupt as hell. When Winnie found out, he nearly choked one to death in the White House. To show how sorry they were, these same poker buddies then went around town, roughing up Winnie's many mistresses and burning the incriminating erotic letters he had written them. The most amazing part of all of this was that the American public had no idea it was going on.

Florence, deciding it would be best if her husband got out of DC for a bit, convinced him to take a tour of Alaska and the western U.S. Throughout the trip, Winnie got progressively sicker, probably because he wasn't getting any strange on the regular. By San Francisco he was obviously having major medical problems. However, his wife refused to let him see any doctors except for a homeopathic quack who treated Winnie by repeatedly plunging a hypodermic needle into various parts of his body. Tiring of such bullshit, Winnie had a heart attack and died.

#30 Calvin Coolidge
(1923-1929)
The Quietest Cowboy

Cal, often called Silent Cal because he never spoke, was born to middle class parents who ran a store and a farm. While still a child, his mother died, and his upbringing was mostly left to his crazy ass grandmother who demanded perfection and locked Cal in the attic for days at time when he failed to meet her expectations. This experience made Cal a weird guy, an unexcitable man with a serious demeanor and a bone dry sense of humor. Like most presidents, Cal went to university and became a lawyer. For a wife, Cal married Grace Anna Goodhue. It was a good match. Cal never spoke a word and she never shut up. Grace fell in love with Cal after she peeped into his window and caught him shaving wearing nothing but long johns and a derby hat. She thought it was hilarious, which seems an odd reason to decide to marry someone. Grace was a teacher for the deaf and dumb, and often people would mistake Cal for one of her students. For a wedding gift, Cal gave Grace fifty pairs of socks that needed mending.

Despite lacking in loquaciousness, Cal could be quite an eloquent speaker when he chose to be. This helped him when he decided to get into politics, slowly working his way up to national office. What didn't help him was the fact that he didn't swing his arms when he walked. Despite this peculiarity, he was chosen to run for Vice President in 1920 because everyone just kind of assumed that he was probably an okay guy. Two years into Cal's tenure as Vice President, President Winnie up and died. Cal was off visiting the family farm at the time, so his father, who was a justice of the peace, woke up him at 2:30 AM and administered the oath of office. Cal then went back to sleep.

Cal carried out his presidential duties by pretending that he wasn't president. He avoided doing as much as possible when it came to running the country, and when people came to talk to him, he just sat silently until they felt uncomfortable and left. For some odd reason, Cal did allow people to bring him costumes, which he would willingly put on for photographs. These costumes included a Sioux war bonnet and a full cowboy costume, including a ten gallon hat and chaps with his name on them. Cal kept the hat and wore it while riding a mechanical horse he had installed in his dressing room for exercise. Once, while staying at a hotel, Cal awoke to a burglar in his room. Instead of calling for help, Cal talked to the burglar for several hours and then loaned him 35 bucks. In 1924, Cal was elected to be president again. Not long after, his son died from an infected blister, an event that somehow made Cal even more silent. It also caused him to become slightly unhinged. Cal spent his second term playing pranks on the White House staff, throwing temper tantrums, and forcing the maid to rub Vaseline on his head while he ate breakfast.

Cal chose not to run for president again in 1928, mostly because as he put it, he hated the job. In retirement, he spent most of his time writing his memoirs, preparing a weekly newspaper column, and racing around in his speedboat. In 1932, people tried to get him to run for president again, but he politely told them to fuck off. However, they did convince him to give a speech supporting President Bertie. The speech lasted 30 minutes. Cal died soon after of a heart attack, probably brought on by the exertion of talking for so long.

#31 Herbert Hoover
(1929-1933)
America's Rich Uncle

Bertie had a tough luck childhood. By the time he was nine years old both his parents were dead. Luckily for him, various family members took him in, by which we mean they used him for veritable slave labor, working his ass off, and then shipping him on to the next relative. This practice ended when he was shipped across the country to his uncle, a man who apparently couldn't afford the train ticket to send him back. Bertie's uncle, a man with an endless supply of stumps on his farm, decided that Bertie would be better off removing said stumps than going to school. Luckily, Bertie apparently didn't sleep, attending night school for his education. Deciding that his life could be better, for some unknown reason, Bertie decided to go to university. This dream was nearly dashed when he failed his entry exams, but he was still allowed in because the examiner found him so gosh darn charming. History does not record exactly what that means.

Bertie graduated with a degree in geology and soon after took a job at a mine in Australia. Here, he started some Mad Max shite, manipulating the other employees to oust his boss because that's how business works in Australia. For this, his company gave him a promotion and sent him to China. To celebrate, Bertie sent a telegram to his college girlfriend, Lou Henry, asking her to marry him, a proposal method she was apparently totally cool with. Bertie was damn good at mining, so good that he became a millionaire by age 40. Growing bored with turning rocks into a shit ton of money, Bertie shifted gears and started several relief charities for war torn Europe. This led to him getting appointed to several government positions, which in turn led to literally everyone wanting him to be president. Bertie happily obliged and won the election in 1928.

Who would have thought that it probably wouldn't be that good of an idea to make some random rich guy with zero political experience president? Soon after being elected, the country fell into the Great Depression. Bertie responded by doing nothing and using the Army to attack veterans who dared to ask for their government pensions. While the world went to hell, Bertie hosted extravagant seven course meals at the White House (which always included sweet potatoes with marshmallows), traded sexy banter with his wife in Chinese, and played Hooverball (a game he made up involving people throwing a medicine ball at each other). A bit of an elitist, Bertie insisted that all the White House servants be the same height and that they never be seen. When he walked into a room the servants had to hurriedly hide in closets or around corners, hoping they didn't accidentally step on one of two alligators Bertie let roam freely in the White House. During his presidency Bertie did get hundreds of towns named after him. Unfortunately, they were all shantytowns. Surprisingly, he did not win re-election in 1932.

Following his presidency, Bertie spent most of his time fly fishing, writing books, and writing books about fly fishing. He and his wife would go on long aimless drives to the middle of nowhere, which seems gutsy considering how many people disliked him. Bertie also worked with several aid charities, bad mouthed President Frank every chance he got, was nominated for the Nobel Peace Prize five times, and held the record for the largest bonefish ever caught in Florida. At age 90, doctors removed a tumor from Bertie's intestine. They must have done a bang up job, because not long after, he died from internal bleeding in his gut.

#32 Franklin D. Roosevelt
(1933-1945)
The Man Who Would Be King

Frank was born to rich bored parents who didn't bother to get around to naming him for seven weeks. Frank was home schooled until the age of 14, after which he went to the finest schools his family's money could buy, where he was at best a C student. Growing bored with school, he dropped out of university, and, again with his family's money, entered politics. It was around this time that Frank took the honorable approach of marrying his fifth cousin, Eleanor Roosevelt. Frank's mother didn't approve of the match and showed it by pretty much dominating every aspect of the newlyweds lives, including raising their children and overseeing their finances, even giving the couple a monthly allowance. Frank, being a bit of a momma's boy, just went along with it. This lasted until his mother died in 1941.

Frank and Eleanor's marriage was not an easy one, even without the domineering mother-in-law aspect. Eleanor hated sex and Frank liked it so much he did it with a lot of other women. Despite this, they still somehow managed to have several children. Things got really rocky when Eleanor discovered Frank was in love with her secretary, a woman named Lucy Mercer. Eleanor offered to step aside and give Frank a divorce, but his mother made them stay together, probably because the thought of not torturing Eleanor was too much for her. Though the pair remained married, they never lived together again. A compromise was reached. Eleanor started hanging out with prominent lesbians and Frank's lusts were sated by a bout of polio that paralyzed him from the waist down. Unable to monger whores any longer, Frank threw his passions into politics and stamp collecting. He excelled at both, collecting over a million stamps and getting himself elected president in 1932.

As president, Frank fought the Great Depression using what he himself called policies similar to the economic reforms of fascist Italy. In 1936, he easily won re-election thanks to a campaign of union thugs and threats that everyone would lose their government sponsored jobs if they voted for the other guy. This strategy worked again in the election of 1940 and again in the election of 1944. World War II basically allowed Frank to nationalize everything. Despite being extremely busy, Frank always took time to keep up on his favorite hobbies; collecting stamps, watching Mae West movies, having the IRS and FBI investigate his enemies, snorting cocaine for a "sinus condition", and ordering his bodyguards to beat the shit out of anyone who tried to take photos of him in his wheelchair. Frank also arrested all of the Japanese people in the country, pretended that the holocaust wasn't happening, tried to stack the Supreme Court, and ordered the White House servants to segregate themselves by race.

Despite his health starting to fail early in his third term, Frank was pretty much convinced he should be president forever. As he got sicker, he asked Eleanor to move back in with him, a request which she flatly refused. Instead, Frank's daughter, always one to stir the pot, hooked her father back up with his old mistress, Lucy Mercer. Lucy convinced Frank to get his portrait painted. Right in the middle of sitting for his portrait, Frank complained of a terrible headache, slumped over, and died of a stroke. Not long after his death, an amendment was added to the constitution limiting how many times a person could be president.

#33 Harry S. Truman
(1945-1953)
The "S" Stands For Shut The Fuck Up

What can you say about Harry? Harry thought he was the coolest guy ever, but everyone else thought he was an asshat. He was born to middle class asshat parents who didn't even bother to send him to school until he was eight years old, but forced him to get up at 5 AM every day to practice the piano. Harry didn't go to university. Instead, he tried to join the Army, but was rejected because he was blind as a bat. Harry then worked a series of clerical jobs where he was paid so little that he had to live in a hobo camp. When World War I broke out, Harry cheated his way into the Army by memorizing all the eye charts. The Army then put his blind ass in charge of artillery. Harry spent most of the war showing off his wide range of hobo profanities.

Harry was in love with his childhood friend Bess Wallace. When he asked her to marry him, she said no, which to Harry meant, "pester me until I say yes." She finally gave in, which was lucky for Harry since it allowed him to move into his new mother-in-law's house, which was needed given that he had recently lost all of his money in a failed haberdashery business. Unfazed, Harry went into politics. Being a foul mouthed hick worked amazingly well for Harry, and he won a series of elections which culminated with him becoming Vice President in 1944. However, President Frank wasn't a big fan of his new VP. Consequently, the two almost never met or talked. Harry was relegated to a role of mostly playing the piano to entertain the troops.

The not so sudden death of President Frank elevated Harry to the presidency. Harry, not knowing what to do, probably because he had never been briefed on anything, pretended to be Frank for the next three years. People liked Frank, so it went over quite well. In 1948, Harry ran for president, an election nobody thought he could win, not even his own wife. Harry, unperturbed, rode a train around the country, cursing at people at every stop. After winning the election, Harry decided it was time to be himself. Unfortunately, himself turned out to be an incompetent crazy person who constantly lost his temper. Harry spent his second term fighting communists (both real and imagined), asking his mother for advice on how to be president, and writing angry letters to newspapers who dared to suggest that his daughter's singing was shitty.

Nobody wanted Harry to run again in 1952, so instead he went back to his mother-in-law's house and retired. Harry was completely broke, having spent all of his salary on tailored suits, brightly colored shirts, and bowties. Most of the early days of Harry's retirement was spent taking out loans and writing his memoirs. Embarrassed by his poverty, the U.S. government created a pension for ex-presidents. When Medicare was created Harry was given the first card. The free government healthcare did the trick. Harry went into the hospital to be treated for pneumonia, where he died from all his organs simultaneously failing.

#34 Dwight D. Eisenhower
(1953-1961)
My True Love Is A Flag

Duckpin, named after a game somewhat similar to bowling that he played all the damn time, was born into a poor family of Jehovah's Witnesses. Duckpin was originally named David, but after trying it out for a bit, his mother decided that David was a stupid name and that he should be named Dwight. Finding Dwight too hard to remember, she then just started calling him Ike for short, a name she liked so much that she just started using it for all of his siblings as well. When your mother calls you and all of your brothers the same name, you often find ways to differentiate yourself. Duckpin did this by spending his childhood hanging out with an illiterate hobo who taught him how to fish and play cards. Duckpin's family were pacifists, so naturally he joined the Army and went to West

Point. He spent most of his time there ignoring his studies and playing every sport possible, except for baseball.

After leaving West Point, Duckpin went on vacation and met a woman named Mamie Doud. He apparently decided that she was good enough because he married her a few months later. When they exchanged vows, Duckpin let Mamie know that she would always come in second in his book behind the good old U.S.A. He then proceeded to drag her around the country for 35 years, moving about once a year. For some reason, theirs was not a happy marriage. Despite having never been in actual combat, when World War II broke out Duckpin got made leader of all Allied armies in Europe. This probably had nothing to do with the fact that he often let his superiors win at cards. Becoming the top general had its perks, such as a British fashion model for a personal driver. The two of course had an affair, though it wasn't a very salacious one considering Duckpin couldn't get his flag to full staff. Despite this, Duckpin wanted to marry his mistress/driver. Like a good soldier he asked his superiors for permission to get a divorce. They said no.

After the war, everyone wanted Duckpin to be president. He declined to run in 1948, but gave in and won by a landslide in both 1952 and 1956. Duckpin spent most of his presidency fighting communists (again, both real and imaginary), making sure his three lucky coins were always in his pocket, painting so-so portraits of his wife (his general attitude towards her probably didn't help), and playing a ridiculous amount of golf. Duckpin loved golf so much that he had a putting green installed at the White House. When squirrels started tearing up his putting green, he ordered the Secret Service to shoot them. Duckpin was not a healthy man. During his presidency he suffered a heart attack and a stroke, both of which incapacitated him for a time.

Duckpin spent his post-presidency years mostly continuing his never ending quest of perfecting his golf game and painting pictures that even he said were shit. He also worked on his memoirs, which for some strange reason did not include mention of that time during the war when he was unable to get an erection. Duckpin's health continued to fail, resulting in several more heart attacks, until it finally just gave up. Duckpin's last words were, "I want to go, God take me." Duckpin's one regret for his entire life was that he had never played baseball while at West Point.

#35 John F. Kennedy
(1961-1963)
Sex Addict

Let's just get it out of the way. This man was most definitely some kind of sex robot sent from the future to make love to as many women as humanly possible. The guy couldn't go three days without getting some strange. Anyways, Sexotron Model JFK69 was born to an extremely wealthy family headed by his father Joe; a bootlegging, womanizing, Nazi sympathizer; who raised all of his sons with the specific aim of making at least one of them president. He also lobotomized one of his daughters, but that's another story not covered in this illustrious document. Sexotron was a sickly child. He was always in and out of school due to some disabling malady. By the time he turned 37, he had been given last rites three times. His health problems were not helped by the fact that one of his legs was shorter than the other, resulting in a life time of back trouble.

When World War II broke out, Sexotron was in too poor of health to join the military, but his rich dad's friends got him into the Navy and made him the captain of a PT boat in the South Pacific anyway. This PT boat promptly got run over by a Japanese destroyer. After the war, Sexotron, on his father's insistence (and money), got into politics. To help his political career, Sexotron married a newspaper photographer named Jackie Bouvier. This in no way slowed down Sexotron in his mission to pork everything that moved. Jackie, being a good political wife, turned a blind eye and bad mouthed him in French. In 1960, Sexotron fulfilled his father's dream and ran for president, winning because America found him just so damn charming and handsome.

A lot of stuff happened while Sexotron was president, but he probably didn't remember quite a bit of it given that he was always wiped out on pain medications. For Sexotron, the presidency was a never ending soiree; booze and marijuana with the rich and famous, flings with socialites and movie stars, naked pool parties with an army of secretaries and interns (many of whom had no official duties other than satiating Sexotron's unending lusts), and so on. When not sexing it up, Sexotron spent his time sailing, reading James Bonds books, taking his personal bathroom scale on every trip, doodling during important meetings, trying to learn French (so he could understand what his wife was saying about him), secretly recording every conversation in the Oval office, and smoking 4 to 5 cigars a day. Sexotron also promoted children's fitness, though it was probably just to ensure he wouldn't have to sleep with any fatties 20 years in the future.

Unfortunately, as they all do, Sexotron's party came to an end. Despite being extremely charming, there were a lot of people who did not like him. In the three years he was president, there were four assassination attempts on his life, one of which involved being stalked by a crazy man with a car full of dynamite. The fourth nut job did the trick. Sexotron was killed by a gunshot to the head while riding around in his limousine with the top down.

#36 Lyndon B. Johnson
(1963-1969)
Dick Waving Psychopath

Who was Uncle Cornpone? A dick waving psychopath, that's who. Uncle Cornpone was a paranoid manic-depressive. Uncle Cornpone was the president 1960's America deserved. Born to shit poor parents, Uncle Cornpone was an awkward talkative child whom his grandmother predicted would end up in prison. In the eleventh grade he was elected class president, which put the idea in his head of becoming the real thing. He spent the rest of his crazy life striving for that goal. The first thing any good president needs is a wife, so Uncle Cornpone hounded Claudia Taylor until she agreed to marry him. He then made her change her named to Lady Bird so she'd have the same initials as him. Of course, he gave all their children the same initials as well. Hell, even the dog was given a name with the initials LBJ.

Politics is a game of wit and wiles, but Uncle Cornpone had neither, so instead he dominated people by giving them what became known as the Johnson Treatment, which involved Uncle Cornpone invading someone's personal space, leaning way in, waggling his eyebrows, and constantly changing the volume of his voice at unpredictable intervals from whisper to scream. If that didn't do the trick, Uncle Cornpone would just pull out his dick, which he affectionately called Jumbo. It was a political career fueled by spitting, cursing, and 60 cigarettes a day. When Uncle Cornpone had a heart attack and had to quit smoking, he just doubled down on the spitting and cursing. This somehow led to him bad mouthing his way to being Sexotron's VP. Neither man was a big fan of the other. When Sexotron got shot, Uncle Cornpone got his dream. He was finally president.

Despite being president, Uncle Cornpone never forgot his humble origins. The man peed whenever the notion took him, no matter where he was, or who was around him. He once even peed on the leg of one of his Secret Service agents. During meetings, when Uncle Cornpone had to have a bowel movement, he didn't stop the meeting. Instead, he forced people to come into the bathroom with him. When he wasn't happy, he would belch and fart to show his displeasure. Uncle Cornpone's diplomatic style began and ended with his dick. He'd often skinny dip with visiting dignitaries to establish what he called genital domination. When dick politics failed to work, Uncle Cornpone would resort to physical violence, once even assaulting the Prime Minister of Canada. When he wasn't waving his dick around, Uncle Cornpone kept busy sticking it in every White House secretary he could get his hands on, something his wife was not only okay with, but almost encouraged. Despite what the above may suggest, Uncle Cornpone was a very hygienic man. He forced the White House plumber to spend five years designing a special shower which shot high pressured jets of water right at Jumbo and right up Uncle Cornpone's ass. We're not sure what he named his ass.

After being elected for his own term in 1964, Uncle Cornpone decided not to run again in 1968. The day he left office he took back up smoking cigarettes, grew his hair out, and started getting fat. Uncle Cornpone's retirement was largely spent writing his memoirs, pretending to drive his car into a lake to freak out visitors, and making random 3 AM phone calls. For reasons not understood by medical science, Uncle Cornpone's health began to deteriorate rapidly, and after months of constant chest pains, he died of a heart attack in his bed, his hand reaching towards the phone for one last late night call.

#37 Richard M. Nixon
(1969-1974)
The Loneliest Boy In The World

Who wants a president who protects the environment, promotes worker safety, and supports affirmative action? Who wants a president who believes in universal healthcare and a guaranteed minimum wage? If you do, then you want Plum. Plum, also called Tricky Dicky and Gloomy Gus, was an awkward, paranoid man who had a face like a Halloween mask. Born to a Quaker family, Plum was never allowed to do anything fun as a child, unless you consider going to church four times on a Sunday fun. While his family was long on religious sentiment, they were short on cash, forcing Plum to make his own way through college, working as a carnie and living in a shack.

Plum fell in love with a woman named Patricia Ryan. He spent long hours writing her gaggingly mushy lover letters. While Patricia did not reciprocate, she did generously let Plum drive her to and from dates in other cities with other men. After two years of this, she caved and finally married him. After college, Plum failed at pretty much every business he tried his hand at, including a venture involving frozen orange juice. Luckily, World War II broke out and Plum got sent by the Navy to the South Pacific, where instead of fighting, he opened a bar and proceeded to steal money from drunken sailors by cheating at cards. By the end of the war, he had raised $100,000 (in today's money) which he used to jump start his political career. An early high of becoming Duckpin's VP, solely because he was definitely not a communist, was dashed by a loss in the 1960 presidential election versus the much more handsome Sexotron.

Despite being the type of man who wore business suits to the beach, Plum somehow convinced America that he wasn't a poorly carved ventriloquist dummy and got elected president in 1968 and again in 1972 (by the widest margin ever). It was a great American story of a self-made man, which Plum ruined by going completely insane. Everything and everybody somehow became involved in a conspiracy to ruin him. Coffee cold that morning? Conspiracy. Failure to pick up a spare (Plum was nuts about bowling)? Conspiracy. Seam of his pants rubbing his undercarriage a little too close? Conspiracy. To combat his many enemies, both imaginary and real, Plum took to recording all of his conversations and forming a special team of goons to dig up dirt on anyone seen as being against him. Somehow this all blew up in Plum's face, and after a series of scandals, most involving recordings of Plum's crazy ramblings, he became the first president to ever resign.

Following his resignation, Plum spent most of his time watching musicals and sitting at his desk and doing nothing. Growing bored of this, he worked to make people love him again, writing his memoirs, hitting the talk show circuit, pretending not to be an anti-Semite, and trying his best to act the elder statesman. Somehow, despite being the most despised man in America, and not even allowing his best friend to call him by his first name, it worked, and accolades began to roll in again. However, it was about this time that Plum's wife died, and heartbroken, he soon followed her with a stroke. Eventually, the world forgot everything about him except for the fact that he was a crazy son of a bitch.

#38 Gerald R. Ford
(1974-1977)
It Was A Good Thing He Was Handsome

Jerry was a bit of a nitwit and probably the closest we've ever come to having John Madden be president. When Jerry was born, he was actually named Leslie, after his father, but a few days later his crazy ass abusive father threatened to kill baby Jerry with a knife, so his mother wisely chose to file for divorce. She later remarried and renamed baby Leslie after his new step-daddy. Jerry was the most American of all the American presidents. He was a literal boy scout, an all-star on his university's football team, and he even did a bit of modeling on the side. When he wasn't busy being athletic and beautiful, he kept busy working summers as a park ranger, feeding the bears. The NFL wanted

Jerry to play professional football, but instead he decided it would be best if he went to law school, where he figured he was less likely to fall down and hurt himself.

When World War II broke out, Jerry joined the Navy and insisted they put him into combat in the South Pacific. After a couple of close calls, the Navy shipped him back home to coach football. After the war, Jerry decided to run for Congress. He was seen as a likable simpleton, something that had nothing to do with the fact that he had played football without a helmet, a man the voters felt was just like them. Jerry campaigned by showing up at various houses and helping farmers milk their cows. During his first election he married a model and dancer named Betty Bloomer. Since she was a divorcee, Jerry didn't marry her until right before election day. Their honeymoon was spent at political rallies. Jerry won that first election, and spent the next 25 years in Congress, a time during which he never introduced a single bill.

Jerry was the only president who was never elected either president or VP. In 1973, VP Spiro Agnew resigned after it was found out that he never paid his taxes. Jerry was chosen to replace him because he was so damn likable. The next year, President Plum resigned, and Jerry was given the top job. Jerry spent most of his time as president doing the same as when he was in Congress, which is to say, nothing. Jerry swam every day, kept close track of college football, and forced the White House marching band to play his alma mater's fight song instead of Hail to the Chief. He mostly stood around smiling like an idiot. The one bright spot of Jerry's presidency was that everyone loved his wife Betty because she was so cheerful, outgoing, and outspoken, though this was probably likely due to her being an alcoholic pill popper.

In 1976, Jerry tried to run for president, but failed to be re-elected because he was so damn boring, oh, also probably because he pardoned Plum. Jerry stayed involved in politics, but spent most of his time golfing with Bob Hope, forcing his wife into treatment for her various addictions, and writing his memoirs (which apparently is a requirement for former presidents). Unlike previous presidents, Jerry didn't have the decency to die soon after leaving the White House, and continued on for another 30 years, giving old fuddy-duddy advice to anyone who would bother to listen. He then finally died of a stroke.

#39 Jimmy E. Carter
(1977-1981)
The Curse Of The Killer Rabbit

Peanut was the first president to be born in an actual hospital. He was then taken from that modern hospital to a house with no electricity and no running water in the Deep South. By all accounts, Peanut was a little shit growing up, stealing from the church collection plate and shooting his sisters in the ass with a BB gun. His father, a peanut farmer, despite the fact that he was an inbred redneck, did his best to increase the family's wealth through a series of schemes. Peanut's father was moderately successful, and to show off, the family installed a dirt tennis court. Peanut was the first member of his family to graduate high school, and deciding it wasn't good enough, joined the Navy, studied nuclear physics, and eventually worked on nuclear submarines. Early in his

Naval career he married his sister's friend Rosalyn Smith, and then drug her around the country from post to post.

Peanut decided that the illustrious career of a Navy officer wasn't for him and resigned so he could return to his father's peanut farm, which was pretty much broke. Peanut had no money, and even had to live in subsidized housing for a time. Peanut farming was not as much fun as Peanut thought it would be, though he did once think he saw an UFO, so he decided to go into politics. While initially not very successful, Peanut started winning after he began to pretend that he was a terrible racist. This success through lying made Peanut decide that he was qualified to be president. In 1976, he ran for president, and despite being a long shot candidate, managed to win thanks to the fact that no one had any idea who he was, so therefore, he must be better than the current crop of lying assholes. It probably didn't hurt that he gave a shocking interview in Playboy magazine where he admitted to the fact that he sometimes thought about naked women who were not his wife.

Peanut entered the White House, taking the oath of office under a giant peanut balloon. He then fretted so much about what he was supposed to do that he ended up doing nothing. About all he accomplished was changing which side of his head he parted his hair on and learning how to speed read. Peanut was a bit of a micromanaging prick. It was so bad that he even personally maintained the schedule for the White House tennis court and bowling alley. Wanting to look like a man of the people, he often had himself photographed carrying his own luggage. The suitcases were actually empty. He also ordered his Secret Service agents to never talk to him or even look at him. Which is probably why they did little to help him when he was attacked by a killer rabbit while out boating, forcing him to fend off the angry critter on his own with a boat paddle. Peanut was not re-elected in 1980, probably because when the economy went to hell he gave a speech that basically said everyone was fucked.

Following his presidency, Peanut went back to his peanut farm, but discovered that he was still pretty terrible at it. To make ends meet, he wrote and sold his memoirs, and when they did well, started writing down whatever shit came into his head. This of course then led to Peanut founding several humanitarian organizations which helped people forget what a shitty president he had been. Peanut is still alive today, though he once almost died of brain cancer. Peanut mostly spends his time bad mouthing every single one of his successors, meeting with foreign dictators (whether they want him to or not), and generally pretending that his opinions still matter.

#40 Ronald W. Reagan
(1981-1989)
America's Forgetful Grandpappy

Ronnie was basically America's granddad. Born to a lower middle class family, his father, who worked as a salesman, didn't even bother taking his wife to the hospital for the birth of his son, instead opting to let the baby be born right there in their second floor apartment. Ronnie's father gave him the nickname Dutch, because he thought Ronnie looked like he was Dutch. Ronnie was not of Dutch descent. It was a different time. Ronnie studied economics at university, but was a pretty piss poor student. The only smart thing he did in college was work as a dishwasher at a sorority. After college, Ronnie really didn't feel like getting a job, so instead he became an actor in crummy movies. It was during this time that he met and married fellow actor Jane Wyman. When

World War II broke out he was drafted, but due to having poor eyesight, he was kept stateside where he acted in crummy training films.

After the war, Ronnie went back to making B-list movies in Hollywood, but eventually gave it up to head up the actor's union. He mostly used his position to rat out fellow actors with communist sympathies. This kept Ronnie so busy that his wife divorced him because he didn't have enough time to carry out his marital duties. Luckily, Ronnie had just met an actress named Nancy Davis, who had been confused with another communist supporting actress with the same name, so he didn't remain unmarried for long. The two were deeply in love, and Ronnie often called her by the pet name Mommy, which is pretty weird. Soon after getting together the pair saw a UFO. Fearing an alien invasion, Ronnie decided to get into politics. This decision culminated in him running for president three times, finally beating President Peanut in 1980, not because anyone really liked him, but because nobody liked President Peanut.

Ronnie was the oldest man ever elected president, and he acted pretty much the way you'd expect an old man would act. He spent most of his time as president complaining about taxes, being scared of communists, feeding the squirrels, sending personal checks to anyone who would write to him about their money problems, worrying that all the kids were on drugs, relaxing in sweat pants, making grandfatherly jokes, and making sure there were always plenty of jelly beans in the White House. Soon after being elected, a crazy man shot Ronnie to impress the actress Jodie Foster. Ronnie survived, which left Jodie Foster less than impressed. Ronnie was re-elected in 1984, after which he promptly began developing dementia. Aliens were always at the forefront of Ronnie's mind. Every chance he got he warned his aides and foreign dignitaries of the possibility of an impending space invasion. Unfortunately for Ronnie, nobody really paid much attention to his ravings, probably because in most cases he was unable to recall the names of the people he was talking to. Nancy, not to be out done, got really into astrology, and began using the positions of the planets to advise her husband.

After leaving the White House, Ronnie spent most of his time riding horses and trying to convince people that a person should be allowed to be president for more than two terms. Ronnie's dementia grew into full on Alzheimer's, leaving him a forgetful husk of a man who was in no way capable of saving us from the UFO threat. Ronnie lived in his own world for more than a decade, having no idea what was happening around him, which is okay, because not much of it was really that great. Ronnie finally died of pneumonia.

#41 George H.W. Bush
(1989-1993)
Poppy Knows Best

Poppy, so called because even as a child he acted like everybody's dad, was born to a wealthy Wall Street family. Poppy was raised in the most preppy way possible. We're talking about the kind of preppy that involves tennis in the afternoon with a guy named Thadwyk whilst wearing an argyle sweater tied around your shoulders. When World War II broke out, Poppy joined up, but not with the Army, that was for poor folks, but with the Navy Air Wing. While a pilot, he named his planes after his high school sweetheart, Barbara Pierce. By the end of the war there had been three Barbara's. After leaving the Navy, Poppy returned home and married the real Barbara, a woman who even at a young age looked old enough to be his mother. Poppy went to university, mostly to play baseball, and then threw out all that book learning, and his family's money, to become a self-made oil tycoon. Poppy went from living in a duplex where his family had to share a bathroom with two hookers, to a millionaire by age 40.

Like many self-made men, Poppy decided that making a bunch of money gave him the right to tell others how to live their lives. Poppy got into politics and quickly learned that he wasn't very good at it. He won some and lost some, but never really seemed to get very far ahead. Poppy's luck changed in 1974 when he told President Plum he should resign, which Plum did three days later. Poppy was then sent to China to keep him from making such suggestions to other powerful politicians. This didn't faze Poppy, who took up bike riding. Poppy then enjoyed a series of other political appointments, including UN ambassador and head of the CIA, which culminated in him becoming President Ronnie's Vice President. In 1988 Poppy was elected president, mostly because his opponent was a ridiculously tiny man.

Poppy's first proclamation upon becoming president was to ban broccoli from the White House. Poppy's mother had made him eat broccoli as a child, even though he hated it. Instead of broccoli, Poppy ate pork rinds. Poppy then bought a dog to be his new best friend and gave the dog its own room. Poppy preferred being a low key president, avoiding announcing any long-term goals for the country. Instead, he golfed at rapid speeds, went hunting, gave out awards to people who fell asleep in meetings, hosted horseshoe tournaments, and tried to train his beloved dog to use an automatic dog biscuit dispenser. Poppy's foreign policy mostly involved going to war with random tin pot dictators and throwing up on the prime minister of Japan, probably because the prime minister tried to force him to eat broccoli.

In 1992, Poppy failed in his bid to be re-elected because even though Americans love quick and dirty wars, they hate recessions. The fact that Poppy was confused by a grocery checkout scanner probably didn't help. Poppy and Barbara moved in with some friends, who were not prostitutes, until they could get their own house built. In retirement, Poppy, a stuffy man, allowed himself one piece of fun in that he started wearing crazy dress socks. He also took up skydiving and continued hunting. As he got older, he became confined mostly to a wheelchair, so he started shooting things from the pickup like some kind of redneck. Poppy spent his elder years jumping out of airplanes, having aircraft carriers named after him, and grabbing random women's asses. Old as balls, he eventually died of Parkinson's Disease.

#42 William J. Clinton
(1993-2001)
Pretty Much A Used Car Salesman

Bubba's dad was a travelling salesman named William Blythe who spent most of his time seducing women. Bubba's mama was Blythe's fourth wife. The previous three marriages, two of whom were sisters, ended because of his roving eye. Three months before Bubba was born, Blythe died in a car accident. His mother reacted to this tragedy by leaving her newborn son with her parents and going to nursing school. Bubba's grandparents were strong disciplinarians who forced him to learn how read by age three. After nursing school, Bubba's mama returned and re-married. This time to an alcoholic abusive used car salesman named Roger Clinton. For some reason Bubba decided he should look up to the man and legally changed his last name to Clinton. It wasn't long before he bought an El Camino and put AstroTurf in the back.

Bubba was an excellent saxophone player and planned on being a professional until he met President Sexotron, who showed him you could get laid just a much being in politics. Bubba went to law school, dodged the draft by going to England, smoked marijuana but did not inhale, and got married to Hillary Rodham after being turned down by her a couple of times. Once out of college, Bubba went into politics, something he turned out to be rather good at despite his propensity for involving himself in real estate scams and groping any woman who dared to let herself get within reach. Bubba was white, good looking, and charming, meaning he could pretty much get away with anything. This charisma led him to getting elected president in 1992 and re-elected in 1996.

Bubba might have been president, but he was also still a redneck. He and his wife often had loud fights, full of cursing and throwing things. Both were described as paranoid. Bubba loved going jogging to improve his health, though this was probably a moot point given that his jogs always ended at McDonalds. For Bubba, a healthy meal was a tall glass of Kool-Aid and a whole apple; core, seeds, stems, and everything. During his presidency, Bubba continued having affairs, the most famous of which was with a chubby 22 year old intern named Monica Lewinsky. When Hillary found out about the affair she hit Bubba with a lamp. When the U.S. government found out, Bubba lied about it, and then tried to distract the nation by ordering the military to bomb Africa. This led to Bubba getting impeached for perjury and America learning all sorts of interesting facts about stained blue dresses and where Bubba liked to put his cigars. Despite it all, Bubba prevailed, avoiding impeachment, setting a legal standard that fellatio is not sex, and redefining the word "is."

When Bubba and Hillary left the White House, they stole pretty much anything they could get their hands on and trashed everything else. Not being fans of Bubba's successor, they also left obscene messages on all the phones and stole all the W's from the computer's keyboards. Bubba has spent his retirement writing his memoirs, golfing, working the public speaking circuit, and supporting Hillary with her own political ambitions, which pretty much began the moment his ended. Bubba is still alive today, probably getting into all sorts of shenanigans.

#43 George W. Bush
(2001-2009)
Why Won't Daddy Love Me?

Dubya was born into an aristocratic family where his father was away most of the time making money. His mother raised him and his siblings in the aristocratic fashion of disciplinary slaps and heated competitions for her love. Like many children, Dubya became rebellious in his college years. God only knows why. Since his family was a bunch of preppy wasps, this involved him becoming a drunken redneck lout. College age Dubya was later described as John Belushi in Animal House without the class. Despite these antics, Dubya graduated with a degree in business, avoided the draft by joining the Texas National Guard, and then went into the oil business.

The oil business did not work out well for Dubya, probably because he had put his amateur college drinking days behind him and had moved on to being a truly professional alcoholic. In polite terms, Dubya was a wayward soul. In real terms he was arrested three times for drunk in public, drunk driving, and stealing a Christmas wreath. He also once challenged his father to a fist fight. To put it bluntly, the man had daddy issues. If he had been born a girl he probably would have ended up being a stripper. Moving on from oil, Dubya became a part owner of a Major League Baseball team, where his drinking was less of a liability. It was at this time that he met Laura Welch at a barbeque. She put an end to Dubya's hijinks. The pair got married and she forced him to sober up and go to church. Having a lot of extra time now that he wasn't drunk 24/7, Dubya decided to go into politics, a move that led him to running for president in 2000.

Dubya won the election thanks to a combination of pretending to be stupider than he actually was, helped along by his shitty public speaking skills, and poorly designed ballots. The fact that his opponent had the charisma of piece of wood in a fancy suit didn't hurt either. Dubya was an authoritarian by nature, and though America was a democracy, the White House was a dictatorship. Everything from Dubya's early bedtime to the length of women's skirts was strictly regulated. Dubya spent most of his presidency being extremely paranoid about terrorists, dancing in the whitest fashion possible, making up somewhat clever nicknames for everyone he met, and taking overly long vacations to his ranch where he spent his free time clearing brush. Hoping to impress his father, Dubya started hanging out with President Poppy's old friends and invaded a country for no good reason. This did not work out well. Dubya was one of the most loved presidents at the start of his presidency, allowing him to get re-elected in 2004, but a hurricane, endless, war, and a financial collapse led to him being the most despised president by the time he left office.

When Dubya left the White House he quietly disappeared, preferring to be out of the limelight except for a few public speaking appearances. With all the brush on his ranch cleared during his presidency, Dubya had to find a new hobby for his retirement. He settled on oil painting. Dubya's paintings tended to focus on portraits of world leaders, dogs, and several of himself naked in the shower and bathtub. Dubya is still alive today, painting like a first year art student and jealously guarding his most prized possession, a photo of him with the band ZZ Top.

#44 Barack H. Obama
(2009-2017)
I Think I'm Awesome, You Should Too

Let's get it out of the way first thing. Barry is an asshole. All of the presidents have been assholes. That's kind of been the point of all this. Barry's father, who was from Kenya, met his mother while they were in university together. Despite already having a wife and two kids back in Kenya, Barry's dad knocked up his mother and then married her. Two years later he left Barry's mother to go knock up and marry other women. The man had a hobby. Barry's mom, not one to let shit get her down, re-married, this time to a dude from Indonesia. Barry spent several years of his childhood living in Indonesia, eating dog and snake and playing with his pet monkey Tata, before getting sent back to the U.S. to live with his grandparents. Money was tight, but thanks to student loans and scholarships, Barry got to go to some of the best universities in the country.

Barry experimented with alcohol and drugs a bit growing up, but spent most of his time playing basketball, listening to disco music, driving around in his rust bucket car, smoking cigarettes, and collecting comic books. While in law school, Barry met his future wife, Michelle Robinson, who just so happened to also be his supervisor. After law school, Barry took a job teaching law. He also got involved in state politics and wrote two autobiographies about how awesome he was. The second autobiography helped propel Barry into national politics, and also allowed him to finally pay off his student loans, four years before getting elected president. In 2008, Barry ran for president on a message of hope, change, and that President Dubya was the worst person ever, much of it delivered via clever internet memes. The strategy worked and Barry won the election.

Barry's presidency mostly consisted of playing golf, sneaking smokes outside, blaming Dubya for practically everything, and pointing out positive statistics even though nobody really felt all that positive about them. Soon after his election, Barry was awarded the Nobel Peace Prize. To celebrate, he kept the U.S. in a state of war throughout his presidency. Barry was great at campaigning for president, but not so good at actually being president. Barry was a man of strong convictions, which is a nice way of saying he didn't know how to compromise. When people disagreed with him, he would become a bit of a jerk, standoffish and condescending, which for some reason didn't make people see things his way. It probably didn't help that he would often give unwanted advice on the best way to carry out mundane activities, such as shaking hands. When Barry was elected president, half the country loved him and half hated him. By the end of his presidency, half still hated him and the other half was just moderately okay with him. For Barry, this was of course totally somebody else's fault.

After leaving the White House, Barry said his main goals were to get his driver's license back and learn how to use a phone newer than a Blackberry. Barry got a taste of his own medicine via his successor blaming everything wrong with the country on him, which might be why his wife became good friends with former President Dubya. In retirement, Barry has done what he does best, writing memoirs about himself. Proving he's the first president who knows how the internet works, he has also started producing Netflix documentaries and hosting a podcast with Bruce Springsteen. Barry is still alive today, undoubtedly sure of himself.

#45 Donald J. Trump
(2017-2021)
Giving America The Bird

Donnie was born to a wealthy upper class family who made sure he had the best of everything, including the best military school when it turned out he was a bit of a turd. His father was a big proponent of the tried and true parenting method of treating your kids like shit, which is probably why Donnie developed some fairly pronounced narcissistic and sociopathic tendencies. Utilizing his daddy's money and connections, as well as every legal loophole and shady business dealing known to humankind, Donnie built up a real estate empire worth millions, at least until the convoluted financial shell game he was playing came crashing down. Not only did he lose millions of dollars, but also his super model wife.

Undeterred, Donnie married a new super model and started suing everyone he knew before they could sue him. He also started slapping his name on everything imaginable, a strategy that somehow eventually made him the star of an extremely popular reality TV show. Now a living brand, Donnie became obsessed with his appearance and public image, which for some reason involved an epic combover and orange spray tan. As a result, he morphed into a parody of himself, a germaphobe desperate for attention, but refusing to be touched. His new super model wife wasn't a fan of this version of him, so he just married a new one, a Slovenian model named Melanija Knavs.

In 2016, Donnie ran for president, probably as part of some kind of get rich scheme. Despite a propensity for shady dealings and unwanted groping, his strategy of waving his dick around, bullying, and lying about everything amazingly worked. Apparently enough Americans were so sick of politics that just burning it all down seemed like a viable solution. Donnie made everyone uncomfortable, but for a lot of people it was the kind of uncomfortable you feel when as a teenager someone flips off your dad and calls him a mother fucker. Everyone was surprised by the victory, especially Donnie, who suddenly had to give up a lucrative TV career for a salary amounting to peanuts. Deciding that his win proved he was some kind of Machiavellian genius, Donnie began governing in a manner best described as the random whims of a cranky toddler mixed with the ravings of your conspiracy loving racist uncle. It was a complete shitshow, fueled by burger binges, late night Tweets, and an extremely distorted vision of reality. Donnie didn't give two shits about anyone but himself, and if that meant destroying even the foundations of American democracy, then so be it. The saddest part was that Donnie saw himself as the good guy, a poor misunderstood soul whom everyone was out to get.

Donnie lost his bid for re-election in 2020, though of course being Donnie, he completely refused to accept it, declaring the entire thing to be a fraud and inciting a mob to attack the U.S. Capitol building. This led to him getting kicked off of nearly all social media and becoming the first president to ever be impeached twice. His desperation to win re-election probably had nothing to do with the fact that once back in the private sector he would have to deal with a growing pile of debts, lawsuits, and possible criminal charges. Today, Donnie is hiding out in a compound in Florida, plotting away on how he can get his ass elected president again in 2024.

#46 Joseph R. Biden
(2021-????)
Just Sit There And Keep Quiet

Sleepy Joe was the son of a devout Catholic used car salesman and had a terrible stutter throughout his childhood, something he tried to cure by reciting poetry with pebbles in his mouth. Not the brightest bulb in the box, he was a C- average student clear through college, always just squeaking by. While still in college, he met a teacher named Neilia Hunter, who he somehow convinced to marry him despite the fact that she often had to slip him $20 bills under the table to pay for dinner during their dates. Neilia's parents weren't really down with the wedding, not because Sleepy Joe was broke, but rather because he was Catholic, it was a different time. After law school, Sleepy Joe worked as a public defender for a few years, but deciding working sucked, soon after ran for public office. Though continually putting his foot in his mouth, he somehow got elected to the U.S. Senate at the age of 29, making him one of the youngest Senators in U.S. History. Something his wife and daughter celebrated by getting killed by a truck hauling corncobs while buying a Christmas tree.

Apparently having an education fetish, Sleepy Joe married a second teacher named Jill Jacobs, and hunkered down in the Senate for the next four decades. Spending his time giving rambling poorly worded speeches, jumping motorcycles, trying to be everybody's friend, and inappropriately touching women, though less in a sexual way and more in a creepy stepdad wanting to make a connection kind of way. This probably had nothing to do with the fact he shared a bunk bed with his uncle while a child. In 1988, Sleepy Joe ran for president, but soon after had to drop out because he plagiarized his speeches and falsely claimed he had marched for civil rights. Not taking the loss well, Sleepy Joe did not run for president again until 2008, again losing because he was about as exciting as creamed corn. However, he did get to be President Barry's VP, because he was a moderate white guy. The two men did not really get along, with neither speaking to each other for months at a time. In 2016, he was convinced not to run for president because he was seen as being too old, too boring, and too prone to vomiting out random words.

After four years of President Donnie, voters decided that a goofy old man is just what America needed. Winning election in 2020, he became the oldest ever president at the age of 78. So starts the presidency of yet another jerk. What will the future hold? We'll just have to wait and see.

Professor Errare Presents....40 American Jackasses Worth Knowing

American history is full of jackasses, unfortunately many of them have been forgotten. Professor Errare proudly presents forty of them that are well worth remembering.

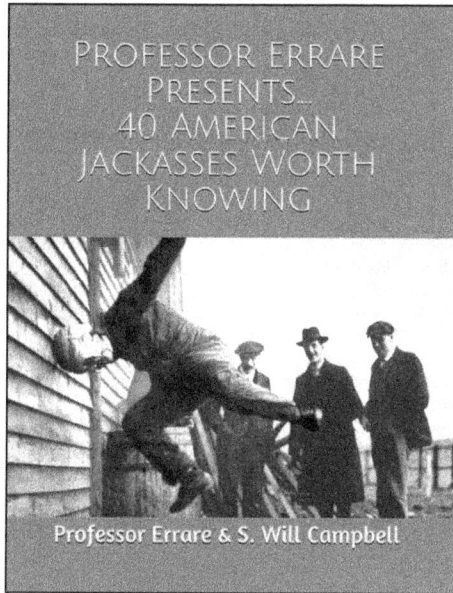

Professor Errare Presents....And Then What Happened

Hey have you heard about that famous event....well guess what, that's not the most interesting thing about it. Don't believe us? Check out this shit.

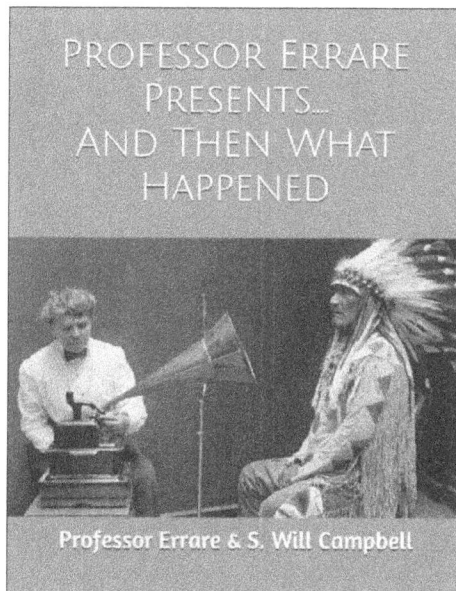

Professor Errare Presents....Random History

Who needs patterns? I'll tell you who doesn't, people who like random history thrown at them with absolutely no rhyme or reason connecting any of it.

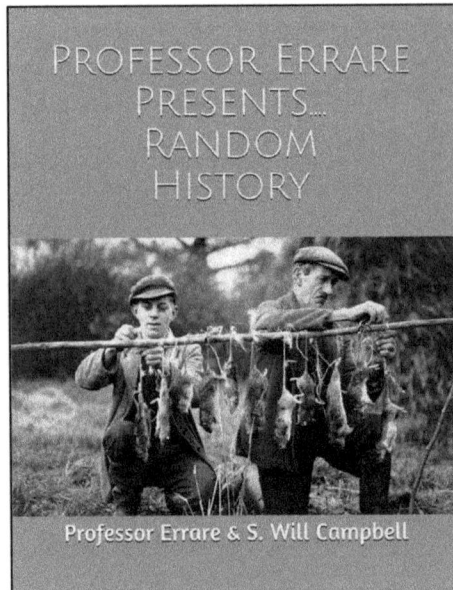

Professor Errare Presents....Stuff You Should Know

The world is a crazy place. There's reasons for that, reasons you should probably know. That stuff is in this book. You should buy this book.

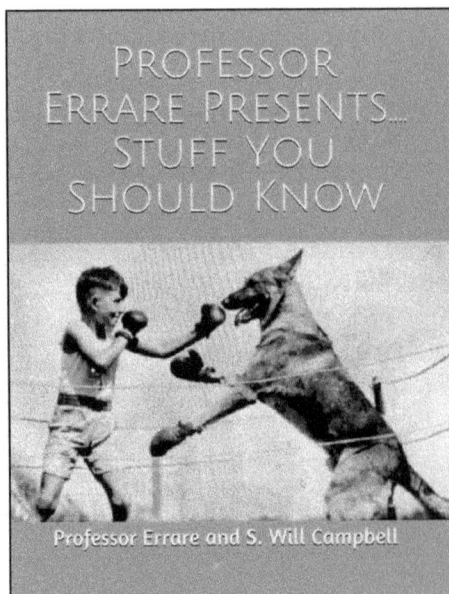

Want more Professor Errare? Are you still thirsty for knowledge? Professor Errare runs a weekly updated Facebook page of the same name with all sorts of tidbits for your perusing. You can find it here:

https://www.facebook.com/professorerrare/

About The Authors

Professor Errare is a world renowned cynic with a degree in bullshit from the University of None Of Your Damn Business. Professor Errare is a proponent of old school history, where the historian does not let things like facts or other opinions get in the way of a good story. Professor Errare hopes that this book generates some income because you can't get coke and hookers for free. He currently runs a blog by the same name where he provides a weekly dose of knowledge.

S. Will Campbell has absolutely no interest in history, but he does know how to type, which is a necessity given that Professor Errare lacks this skill. S. Will Campbell wants nothing to do with Professor Errare, but a collection of sleazy photos that could easily get put on the internet keeps him in line. S. Will Campbell's crippling anxiety keeps him from having a wife and kids, or even pets, but he does have a nice house plant named Morton that keeps him company.

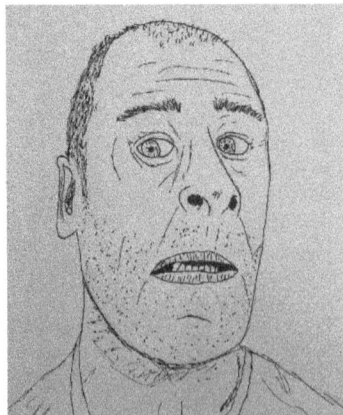

www.ingramcontent.com/pod-product-compliance
Lightning Source LLC
Chambersburg PA
CBHW081634040426

42449CB00014B/3304